MACMILLAN M

D0266068

LEPEN

General Editor: Norman Page

MACMILLAN MODERN NOVELISTS

Published titles

E. M. FORSTER   Norman Page
WILLIAM GOLDING   James Gindin
MARCEL PROUST   Philip Thody
SIX WOMEN NOVELISTS   Merryn Williams
JOHN UPDIKE   Judie Newman
H. G. WELLS   Michael Draper

Forthcoming titles

ALBERT CAMUS   Philip Thody
JOSEPH CONRAD   Owen Knowles
FYODOR DOSTOEVSKI   Peter Conradi
WILLIAM FAULKNER   David Dowling
F. SCOTT FITZGERALD   John S. Whitley
GUSTAVE FLAUBERT   David Roe
JOHN FOWLES   Simon Gatrell
GRAHAM GREENE   Neil McEwan
HENRY JAMES   Alan Bellringer
JAMES JOYCE   Richard Brown
D. H. LAWRENCE   G. M. Hyde
DORIS LESSING   Ruth Whittaker
MALCOLM LOWRY   Tony Bareham
GEORGE ORWELL   Valerie Meyers
BARBARA PYM   Michael Cotsell
MURIEL SPARK   Norman Page
GERTRUDE STEIN   Shirley Neuman
EVELYN WAUGH   Jacqueline McDonnell
VIRGINIA WOOLF   Edward Bishop

MACMILLAN MODERN NOVELISTS
E. M. FORSTER

Norman Page

MACMILLAN

First published 1987

Published by
MACMILLAN EDUCATION LTD
Houndmills, Basingstoke, Hampshire RG21 2XS
and London
Companies and representatives
throughout the world

Typeset by Wessex Typesetters
(Division of The Eastern Press Ltd)
Frome, Somerset

Printed in Hong Kong

British Library Cataloguing in Publication Data
Page, Norman
E. M. Forster.—(Macmillan modern
novelists)
1. Forster, E. M.—Criticism and
interpretation
I. Title
823'.912   PR6011.058Z/
ISBN 0–333–40694–X
ISBN 0–333–40695–8 Pbk

Series Standing Order

If you would like to receive future titles in this series as they are
published, you can make use of our standing order facility. To place a
standing order please contact your bookseller or, in case of difficulty,
write to us at the address below with your name and address and the
name of the series. Please state with which title you wish to begin your
standing order. (If you live outside the United Kingdom we may not
have the rights for your area, in which case we will forward your order
to the publisher concerned.)

Customer Services Department, Macmillan Distribution Ltd
Houndmills, Basingstoke, Hampshire, RG21 2XS, England.

Contents

Acknowledgments

The author and publishers are grateful to Edward Arnold Ltd for permission to reproduce extracts from the following works of E. M. Forster: *Abinger Harvest, Where Angels Fear to Tread, A Room with a View, The Longest Journey, Howards End, The Manuscripts of Howards End* and *A Passage to India*. In addition, the author and publishers would like to thank Alfred A. Knopf, Inc, for permission to reproduce extracts from *Howards End, The Longest Journey, A Room with a View* and *Where Angels Fear to Tread* by E. M. Forster.

General Editor's Preface

The death of the novel has often been announced, and part of the secret of its obstinate vitality must be its capacity for growth, adaptation, self-renewal and even self-transformation: like some vigorous organism in a speeded-up Darwinian ecosystem, it adapts itself quickly to a changing world. War and revolution, economic crisis and social change, radically new ideologies such as Marxism and Freudianism, have made this century unprecedented in human history in the speed and extent of change, but the novel has shown an extraordinary capacity to find new forms and techniques and to accommodate new ideas and conceptions of human nature and human experience, and even to take up new positions on the nature of fiction itself.

In the generations immediately preceding and following 1914, the novel underwent a radical redefinition of its nature and possibilities. The present series of monographs is devoted to the novelists who created the modern novel and to those who, in their turn, either continued and extended, or reacted against and rejected, the traditions established during that period of intense exploration and experiment. It includes a number of those who lived and wrote in the nineteenth century but whose innovative contribution to the art of fiction makes it impossible to ignore them in any account of the origins of the modern novel; it also includes the so-called 'modernists' and those who in the mid- and late twentieth century have emerged as outstanding practitioners of this genre. The scope is, inevitably, international; not only, in the migratory and exile-haunted world of our century, do writers refuse to heed national frontiers – 'English' literature lays claim to Conrad the Pole, Henry James the American, and Joyce the Irishman – but

geniuses such as Flaubert, Dostoevski and Kafka have had an
influence on the fiction of many nations.

Each volume in the series is intended to provide an
introduction to the fiction of the writer concerned, both for
those approaching him or her for the first time and for those
who are already familiar with some parts of the achievement in
question and now wish to place it in the context of the total
oeuvre. Although essential information relating to the writer's
life and times is given, usually in an opening chapter, the
approach is primarily critical and the emphasis is not upon
'background' or generalisations but upon close examination of
important texts. Where an author is notably prolific, major texts
have been selected for detailed attention but an attempt has also
been made to convey, more summarily, a sense of the nature
and quality of the author's work as a whole. Those who want to
read further will find suggestions in the select bibliography
included in each volume. Many novelists are, of course, not
only novelists but also poets, essayists, biographers, dramatists,
travel writers and so forth; many have practised shorter forms
of fiction; and many have written letters or kept diaries that
constitute a significant part of their literary output. A brief
study cannot hope to deal with all these in detail, but where the
shorter fiction and the non-fictional writings, public and private,
have an important relationship to the novels, some space has
been devoted to them.

NORMAN PAGE

To Matthew

1
Life and Career

E. M. Forster's long life – he died in 1970 at the age of ninety-one – witnessed social and cultural changes on an unprecedented scale. When he was born, eminent Victorians such as Tennyson, Browning, Arnold, George Eliot and Trollope were still at work, and he came of age when Victoria was still on the throne. He lived through two world wars; he saw the advent of the nuclear age, the post-1945 transformation of British society, and the granting of independence to India (of whose late imperial period he has given us one of the best-known pictures); and he gave evidence at the '*Lady Chatterley* trial' of 1960, which may be taken as both a symptom and a cause of the new moral climate of the sixties.

We might therefore expect Forster's work to reflect the transformations and upheavals of two or three troubled generations, but such is not the case. Unlike some other long-lived writers such as Tennyson, Hardy and Yeats, his longevity is not matched by a lengthy and continuous period of creativity. He told an interviewer in 1953, 'My regret is that I haven't written a bit more – that the body, the corpus, isn't bigger',[1] and the number of his major works is in fact quite small. Moreover, the six novels that constitute his main claim to attention were all written by the time he was forty-five; indeed, four of them had appeared by the time he was thirty-one, and can be accurately described as Edwardian. The shape of his career, then, is curious and unusual. But quality and influence cannot, of course, be estimated by counting titles or pages, and in some respects Forster's impact on the twentieth century has gone far beyond what his modest output might lead one to expect.

Edward Morgan Forster (always known to his friends as Morgan) was born in London on 1 January 1879. His father,

1

Edward Forster, was an architect who died of consumption
when the baby was only nine months old. His mother, Alice
Clara (usually known as Lily), was to outlive her husband by
some sixty-five years, and Forster remained devoted to her to
the very end. The fatherless boy was brought up in a family
dominated by women: apart from his mother, his wealthy great-
aunt Marianne Thornton, whose biography he later wrote, and
his maternal grandmother Louisa Whichelo were of particular
importance. Forster was later to say that he had spent his
childhood within 'a haze of elderly ladies'.[2]

Soon after the child's fourth birthday, he and his mother
moved to Rooksnest, a pleasant house near Stevenage in
Hertfordshire. Stevenage was not then the 'new town' it has
since become, but was still a small market town surrounded by
fields and farms, and in these peaceful rural surroundings
Forster seems to have spent a happy and secure childhood. The
house itself was later to be portrayed in *Howards End*. Like
many only children whose companions are mainly adults, he
was a precocious boy: not only was he composing long stories
at the age of five, but (as his biographer tells us) 'at the age of
six he took the maids' education in hand', having 'developed a
passion for instructing others'.[3] It was a passion that never left
him. He and his mother were very close to each other and she
was in no hurry to send him to school, but from about the age
of eight he was taught at home by a visiting tutor. At about the
same time his great-aunt Marianne Thornton died, leaving
eight thousand pounds in trust for him – in those days, a
substantial sum. The income from this capital paid for his
education and, as Forster later said, 'made my career as a
writer possible'.

By the time he was eleven, the question of his schooling
could no longer be postponed, and he was sent to a preparatory
school at Eastbourne, where he was unhappy and homesick. In
a letter written to his mother towards the end of the first term,
he shows a remarkable capacity for self-analysis and self-
expression:

I have never been like it before, but it is not at all nice. It is
very much like despondency; I am afraid I shall miss the
train in the morning, afraid you will not meet me, afraid I
shall lose my tickets; these are instances of the kind of state of

mind I am in; ... The worst of school is that you have nothing and nobody to love.[4]

Given the circumstances of the boy's first eleven years, with servants to minister to his needs and a loving mother to bestow on him her almost undivided attention, it is not surprising that the rough and tumble, compulsory games and relatively spartan conditions of boarding-school life proved uncongenial. Lily, like most mothers of her generation, had made no attempt to teach him about sex, and oddly enough he seems to have become only imperfectly informed on the subject during his schooldays; at any rate he said later in his life that 'it was not till he was thirty, by which time he had published three novels, that he altogether understood how copulation took place'.[5] The presentation of women, love, marriage and sexual relationships in his novels needs to be viewed in the context of the early experiences that have been outlined.

When he was fourteen, it was time for Forster to proceed to a public school – an almost inevitable step in his class and period – and his mother made the decision to leave Rooksnest and to move to Tonbridge in Kent, so that he could become a day-boy at the public school there. Lily no doubt believed that, by having him live at home, she could keep an eye on his health and happiness, and she must have been keen to do so for her own sake as well. But as a day-boy in what was primarily a boarding-school Forster found himself in an equivocal and uncomfortable position, and his early years at Tonbridge, until he attained a measure of independence as a senior member of the school, were very unhappy. His depiction of the school as 'Sawston' in *The Longest Journey* is unsympathetic, and he acquired a profound and permanent scepticism concerning the values implanted in the English governing class by the public-school system. As he later wrote in his essay 'Notes on the English Character' (1920):

Solidity, caution, integrity, efficiency. Lack of imagination, hypocrisy. These qualities characterize the middle class in every country, but in England they are national characteristics also, because only in England have the middle classes been in power for one hundred and fifty years. ... For it is not that the Englishman can't feel – it is that he is afraid to feel.

He has been taught at his public school that feeling is bad form. . . . When an Englishman has been led into a course of wrong action, he has nearly always begun by muddling himself. A public-school education does not make for mental clearness, and he possesses to a very high degree the power of confusing his own mind.

The same essay, included in *Abinger Harvest*, declares that the products of the public schools go forth into he world 'with well-developed bodies, fairly developed minds, and undeveloped hearts'; and, as has often been pointed out, the theme of the 'undeveloped heart' is central to Forster's fiction.

In the early novels, English conventionality is often held up for contrast with Mediterranean freedom, and Forster's first taste of continental travel came when he was sixteen, when he and his mother toured Normandy looking at churches during the Easter holidays. But the real turning-point in his early years came in 1897, when he went up to King's College, Cambridge, to read classics (later changing to history). The physical beauty of Cambridge, the freedom and independence of the undergraduate life, and the sense that here was a society intent upon the disinterested pursuit of truth all made a deep and lasting appeal. Above all, he found that it was a community in which personal relationships mattered; for the rest of his life, friendship was to count more than anything else for Forster. Half a century later, one of his closest friends, Joe Ackerley, noted that when arrangements were being made for a birthday dinner to celebrate Morgan's seventieth birthday, he was very upset ('*too* put out over it') when he learned that among the guests on this special occasion would be one who was not in his inner circle of friends. Ackerley commented in his diary:

> as we all know, Morgan has a deep feeling about such matters, an almost mystical feeling, different and more emotional than anything that any of us feel.[6]

The religious term ('mystical') is significant, since the cult of friendship had helped to fill the vacuum caused by Forster's loss of the Christian faith in which he had been brought up.

At King's, friendships were cultivated not only between one undergraduate and another, but between undergraduates and dons, and three men were of particular importance in Forster's development. Oscar Browning, who taught Forster history, was eccentric and snobbish, even absurd; but he cared passionately and sincerely about friendship, and his enthusiasm and energy were infectious. As P. N. Furbank puts it: 'He was not a scholar or thinker; his strength was that, in his sanguine way, be diffused a vision of glory'.[7] A different kind of influence was exerted by Nathaniel Wedd, Forster's classics tutor, who was what would nowadays be called left-wing or anti-establishment. As John Colmer says, Wedd 'undoubtedly helped to form Forster's political and social attitudes, especially his distrust of authority, his sympathy for the outsider, particularly of a lower class, and his hostility to notions of good form'.[8] A third influence was that of Goldsworthy Lowes Dickinson, whose biographer Forster later became: liberal and agnostic, Dickinson was a tireless writer on political subjects and, like Wedd, an ardent advocate of Greek thought.

In his fourth and last year at King's, Forster was elected to the exclusive discussion club known as 'the Apostles'. This had been founded in the early nineteenth century (Tennyson had been one of the earliest members), and met weekly to hear and discuss papers on a variety of topics; its function had been defined by one of its distinguished members, Henry Sidgwick, as 'the pursuit of truth with absolute devotion and unreserve by a group of intimate friends', and the keywords in this statement – truth, devotion, unreserve, friends – are all relevant to Forster's own lifelong commitments. Sidgwick also tells us that 'Absolute candour was the only duty that the tradition of the society enforced', and that 'there was no proposition so well established that an Apostle had not the right to deny or question, if he did so sincerely and not from mere love of paradox'. Lest this sound excessively solemn and earnest for young men of around twenty, it is as well to bear in mind Sidgwick's observation on the prevailing tone of the meetings, that 'suggestion and instruction may be derived from what is in form a jest – even in dealing with gravest matters'. As Colmer points out, this tone is reflected in Forster's own writings, with their 'characteristic blend of gravity and humour'.[9] The opening chapter of *The Longest Journey* is a fictionalised account of a typical meeting of the Apostles.

When Forster left Cambridge in 1901, he decided to postpone

taking up a career. Having read classics and history, he could probably have found employment either in the civil service or in a museum or library, but he already had some thoughts of becoming a writer and his small private income meant that he did not need to start earning a living with any urgency. Instead, he decided to see something more of Europe, and a few months after coming down from Cambridge he set off, accompanied by his mother, on a year's travels, mainly in Italy. Forster seems to have seen his main business as becoming acquainted at first hand with the glories of Italian art: as his mother rather grimly recorded in a letter home, 'We go to churches, pictures and museums daily'. They travelled fairly extensively, going as far south as Sicily; but in a sense it was, as Forster later said, 'a very timid outing', for they stayed in pensions or small boarding-houses and met mainly middle-class English tourists like themselves. They made no Italian friends and never entered an Italian home.

And yet, for all the narrowness and gentility of this timid tour, Forster was genuinely excited by Italy, and it was there that he received authentic inspiration to write his first short story, and hence to begin his career as a creative writer. (As an undergraduate he had contributed a few light essays to student magazines.) The work in question was 'The Story of a Panic', and he describes its origin in the introduction to his *Collected Short Stories*:

> After I came down from Cambridge . . . I travelled abroad for a year, and I think it was in the May of 1902 that I took a walk near Ravello. I sat down in a valley, a few miles above the town, and suddenly the first chapter of the story rushed into my mind as if it had waited for me there. I received it as an entity and wrote it out as soon as I returned to the hotel.

'As if it had waited for me there' is a striking phrase: it is as though, rather than spinning the fiction out of his own brain or experiences, Forster 'found' the story in a particular, ordinary, but also very special place (in the same passage he speaks of 'sitting down on the theme as if it were an anthill'). Places were always to be important to Forster, and his Italian travels provided some of the material for two of his first three novels.

Back in England, he embarked on a little part-time teaching

at the Working Men's College in Bloomsbury, a connection that was to last for some twenty years. (It has been suggested – persuasively, I think – that this experience as an instructor of adult education classes, in which he was called upon to explain fairly complex issues in clear and simple language, had an effect on the style and manner of his writings, especially his essays.) But he was still not ready to settle on a career. From 1903 he published articles and stories in a new progressive monthly, the *Independent Review*, founded and edited by some of his Cambridge friends. He still spent a good deal of time in Cambridge: as early as 22 October 1901, he had written to a friend from Milan, 'I suppose you are now in Cambridge. How I wish – in many ways – that I was too. It's the one place where I seem able to get to know people and to get on with them without effort.' He also remained close to Hugh Meredith, a fellow-Apostle and the most important of the friends of his undergraduate years, and it was apparently during the winter of 1902–3 that Forster and Meredith became lovers. As Furbank says, for Forster the experience was

> immense and epoch-making; it was, he felt, as if all the 'greatness' of the world had been opened up to him. He counted this as the second grand 'discovery' of his youth – his emancipation from Christianity being the first – and for the moment it seemed to him as though all the rest of his existence would not be too long to work out the consequences.[10]

This, the first of Forster's homosexual love affairs, was probably very limited as far as physical expression was concerned, but its effect on him was none the less profound and permanent.

The Greek view of life (the phrase is the title of one of Lowes Dickinson's most popular books), with its endorsement of male friendships as expounded in Plato's *Symposium*, had many advocates in the strictly masculine society of King's, and exerted a strong influence upon Forster. His first sight of Greece was during the Easter vacation of 1903 and there his Italian experience repeated itself, for he again came upon a story – one of his best, 'The Road from Colonus', which he found hanging 'ready for him in a hollow tree'. As with the exuberant outdoor life of Italy, Forster found in Greece a contrast with, and an escape from, the middle-class, puritan, philistine, inhibited life of England, or at least of that part of English society that he belonged to.

In 1904 his mother, who had moved to Tunbridge Wells in 1898, exchanged one genteel small town for another by moving to Weybridge, where she and Forster were to spend the next twenty years. At this time his creative energies were expanding, and he was at work on early versions of what were later to become three novels. Yet it was in other respects a very sheltered life, offering a severely restricted view of human existence, and Forster was aware that a sheer lack of knowledge about how people live was a serious handicap to him as an aspiring novelist. The novel is, as D. H. Lawrence was to put it, 'the book of life', and it is hardly possible to write a novel – certainly not one in the realistic tradition that Forster practised – without a good deal of information and understanding concerning the way in which people of different kinds live their lives. His new year's resolutions for 1905 include, revealingly, 'get a less superficial idea of women' (more easily said than done, as he no doubt realised) and 'don't be so afraid of going into strange places or company. . .', and in 1908 he wrote in a letter to a friend, 'It is the great defect of my position that I only see people in their leisure moments'.[11] Never having known a father or brothers and sisters, he had only a partial knowledge of family life; never having pursued a career, he had no detailed knowledge of any form of employment or of relationships with colleagues or clients; as a homosexual, his knowledge of, and indeed his interest in, half the human race was limited to his mother and other middle-class ladies a generation or two older than himself. None of this stopped him writing fiction; but, as we shall see in discussing his novels, these factors inevitably influenced both what he wrote and what he did not write.

In March 1905 he went for a few months to Germany as tutor to the children of a Prussian landowner who had married an Englishwoman; and it was later in the same year that his first novel was published. *Where Angels Fear to Tread* was favourably reviewed, and he had no reason not to feel encouraged to persevere with writing fiction. Two other novels followed fairly quickly, at intervals of about eighteen months: *The Longest Journey*, his Cambridge novel, in 1907, and *A Room with a View*, his second Italian novel, in 1908. Two years after the latter came *Howards End*. Its reception was, as Philip Gardner has said, a 'solid vote of confidence in Forster's talents': though only thirty-one, he found himself now an established novelist with his reputation 'consolidated and given clearer definition than before'.[12] That the epithet 'Forsterian' was used thus early in his career is a clear indication that he had become identified with a recognisable standpoint: liberal, humane, sceptical, unconventional, relentlessly moral without being ponderous, and even, by the standards of his day, daring, for his mother had been deeply shocked when she read *Howards End* in proof. The appearance of the novel marked, as Furbank says,

> a turning-point in his career, as it did in his life. For the moment he was a celebrity: friends flattered him, newspapers interviewed him, and letters and invitations poured in.[13]

The effect on Forster, however, was to unsettle and disturb him: he disliked popularity, felt curiously guilty and superstitious about his success, and began to fear that his creative talents would dry up. This last was a fear that was to haunt him, not without reason, for many years.

At about this time he seems to have undergone a personal crisis. A few years earlier a second love affair had entered his life, when he met and fell in love with Syed Ross Masood, a young and handsome Indian whom he coached in Latin in preparation for his Oxford entrance. But a major factor in this crisis was his relationship with his mother, who was now well into her fifties and was often depressed and irritable. Summing up the year 1911 in his diary, he described it as 'Terrible year on the whole' and noted that 'pleasure of home life has gone.... Am only happy away from home'.[14] Knowing that, for the sake of his own happiness, he ought to make more of an independent life for himself, he was tormented by guilt at the thought that his mother would have to be more and more excluded from such a life. But his chance to get away, and to have the stimulation of new scenes, was taken in October 1912, when he embarked for India. (His mother travelled with him as far as Naples.) This was the first of three visits to that country: the second was in 1921, when he went for a short period as private secretary to a Maharajah, and the third in 1945 when, elderly and famous, he attended a writer's conference. In India he found the material for his last, and in the opinion of many judges his finest, novel, *A Passage to India*, not completed until much later and published in 1924.

Forster's first four novels had been written quite rapidly, but the record of the years 1912–14 is of uncertainty and loss of self-confidence. By his own account, he began *A Passage to India* in 1912, but soon put it aside. Between September 1913 and July 1914 he produced a version of *Maurice*; the first draft took him only about three months, and before setting to work to revise it he seems to have begun yet another novel, the quickly-abandoned *Arctic Summer*, which survives only as a fragment (written in the spring of 1914). *Maurice*, though finished, was not published and indeed was not publishable, since its treatment of a homosexual theme would have been quite unacceptable in that period. During the next fifty years Forster took it up again from time to time; some of his friends read it, and as late as 1960 he made further substantial revisions and added a 'terminal note' describing its origins and stating that it was now, in the enlightened post-*Chatterley* era, publishable at last. But it did not appear until 1971, a short time after his death.

Maurice was sparked off by a visit to Edward Carpenter, who has been called 'the first modern writer on sex in England'.[15] Carpenter's own voluminous writings are now virtually forgotten, but his influence on various writers, including Forster and D. H. Lawrence, was by no means negligible. Forster acknowledged that he was 'much influenced' by him and, in an essay written after Carpenter's death, referred to his 'cult of friendship' and his 'mingling of the infinite and the whimsical'[16] – phrases that can readily be applied to Forster himself.

When war broke out in August 1914, Forster worked for a time cataloguing paintings in the National Gallery, then went to Egypt, where he spent three years working as a volunteer for the Red Cross. When the war ended, once again back in England, he was active as a journalist – in the years 1919–20 he published the impressive total of 88 essays and reviews – and was for a time literary editor of a left-wing newspaper, the *Daily Herald*. Then came his second visit to India, already referred to, and on his return in 1922 he resumed work on the half-written Indian novel that had been begun some ten years earlier. Work continued throughout 1923, and *A Passage to India* was at last published in June 1924. It was hailed as a masterpiece, and assured Forster a prominent place among living English novelists – though no-one could have foreseen that he would not publish another novel in his lifetime. He was then forty-five, or almost exactly halfway through his long life.

Soon afterwards Forster returned to Cambridge for a time as a fellow of his old college, and in 1927 he delivered a series of lectures on the novel, published as *Aspects of the Novel*. Though informal in tone, they were to have a wide influence in a period when the theory and criticism of fiction was relatively unsophisticated, and they increased Forster's reputation as a man of letters.

During the following years, Forster was certainly not idle: he wrote a good deal of journalism, began to broadcast in 1928 (the BBC having received its charter only in the preceding year), and was active in public life, especially in relation to such issues as censorship and the freedom of the individual. In 1934, for instance, he became the first president of the National Council for Civil Liberties. These activities, in conjunction with his reputation as a writer, established him as a public figure whose low-keyed but strongly-felt utterances were listened to with respect. He had a wide circle of friends, but still spent most of his time at his mother's home in Surrey. And he published no more fiction – indeed, as it turned out, he had permanently abandoned the novel.

We are bound to wonder why Forster wrote no novel after *A Passage to India*, and although the question cannot be conclusively answered it is worth asking, since some of the reasons that may be advanced, in a necessarily speculative way, serve to suggest the nature of his strengths and his limitations as a novelist. The phenomenon is not unique: Thomas Hardy, for instance, abandoned the novel when he was at the height of his powers and was still in his fifties (in the event, he lived for another thirty years or so). But then Hardy had always been a novelist in spite of himself: having secured financial independence as well as fame, he turned back to poetry, his first and truest love, and was active as a poet right until his death. With Forster, on the other hand, one feels that the creative pulse became weak: as Frederick C. Crews said in 1962, 'Forster's literary activity

since 1924 can strike us only as a series of footnotes, however
brilliant, to a career whose real centre lies in the first decade of
the twentieth century'.[17]

As we have seen already, Forster's troubles began much
earlier than 1924: soon after the publication of *Howards End*,
when he was little more than thirty, he was already worrying
about artistic sterility. Furbank, who knew him well in his later
years, suggests that, though a rationalist, he was a deeply
superstitious man, and that the very success of *Howards End*
caused him to be 'afflicted and inhibited by superstitious fears':

> having been especially and royally favoured as a child, he
> had magical feelings about his own life. . . . We can easily
> imagine such a man experiencing irrational fears at the
> realization of very deep wishes.[18]

It was, according to Furbank's reading of the situation, as if ill-
luck or punishment must follow success. This is borne out by a
curious remark that Forster made to T. E. Lawrence after the
great success of *Aspects of the Novel*: 'A sort of nervousness –
glancing at my stomach for beginnings of cancer – seems to
gather in me.'[19]

But there were other and more obvious reasons for Forster's
disinclination to pursue a career that many of his readers must
have felt had only just got into its stride by 1924. When D. H.
Lawrence read *Howards End* in 1915, he wrote to Forster: 'It's a
beautiful book, but now you must go further'; but to 'go further'
was difficult for one whose experience of the world was, as has
already been suggested, fairly narrow. Of all literary forms, the
novel most imperiously demands that a writer be *knowledgeable* –
be well-informed about, for instance, different kinds of social
institution and different human types. Forster's range in his
novels is relatively narrow, he often repeats himself in the
creation of situation and character, and there is a sense in
which he simply ran out of things to say; or, perhaps, what he
had to say was no longer relevant to a world transformed by
the upheavals of the Great War. Another consideration is that,
by 1924, the novel in England had undergone a transformation
that made Forster's kind of novel seem in some respects
distinctly old-fashioned: the earlier works of Joyce, Lawrence,
Virginia Woolf and others were helping, in Ezra Pound's

famous phrase, to 'make it new'. Forster, however, was not by
temperament or talents an innovator on the grand scale: his
novels are closer to Jane Austen and George Eliot than to the
Modernists. Very early in his career, he had staked out a
fictional territory, distinctively individual, in some respects
idiosyncratic, but limited in extent, and he never really went
beyond it so that the experiments and the revolution in the art of
fiction left him behind. Both as a writer and as a man, he matured
very early – or, to put it more accurately, reached a level of
maturity that he did not subsequently proceed very far beyond.
As a result, we can hardly talk of 'development', or 'apprentice
work', 'early', 'middle' and 'late' periods, in connection with
Forster as we can with, for example, Dickens or Conrad or
Lawrence.

A final, and to my mind cogent, reason for Forster's
abandonment of the novel must be added, and that is a growing
impatience with the kind of novel he was expected to write and
had shown the ability to write successfully, and a bitter sense of
disparity between the novels he had written and the ones he
really wanted to write and publish. Forster's novels, at any rate
up to and including *Howards End*, belong to a tradition of fiction
in which the relationships between men and women, and the
rituals of love, courtship and marriage, are of central importance;
but his awareness of his own sexual nature made him
increasingly indifferent to 'the marriage novel'. The other side
of the coin, as Furbank reminds us, is that having written a
homosexual novel, *Maurice*, he was unable to publish it, and this
frustration must have contributed to his disinclination to write
fiction.

He did not, however, stop writing, and the list of his
publications during the last forty or fifty years of his life, mainly
non-fictional, is a long one. Among them are three travel books,
two sparked off by his sojourn in Egypt (*Alexandria: A History
and A Guide* [1922] and *Pharos and Pharillon* [1923]) and one
about India (*The Hill of Devi* [1953]); two biographies, one of
G. L. Dickinson (1934) and one of Marianne Thornton (1956);
and numerous articles and broadcasts, some of which are
collected in two volumes, *Abinger Harvest* (1936) and *Two Cheers
for Democracy* (1951), but many of which remain uncollected. He
was much in demand as a reviewer and lecturer: he gave, for
instance, the Rede Lecture at Cambridge in 1941, published as

Virginia Woolf (1942), and the W. P. Ker Memorial Lecture at Glasgow in 1944, published as *The Development of English Prose between 1918 and 1939* (1945); both are reprinted in *Two Cheers for Democracy*.

Though these constitute, as Crews says, only 'footnotes' to Forster's main achievement as a novelist, they deserve attention, since he had the knack of bringing his personal style and vision to bear upon every task he undertook, even the reviewing of a third-rate book. In the chapters that follow, reference will be made to Forster's non-fictional writings when they seem to throw light upon the novels; for the moment a single example will suffice. In 1925, he reviewed Sir Sidney Lee's biography of Edward VII, a pious and flat-footed official life. Forster begins uncompromisingly, 'This book is dead', and goes on to demonstrate the author's 'incredible pomposity' by drawing attention to the turgidity of his style. His deflation of pretentiousness by means of an image, semi-comic but deadly in its appropriateness, is very characteristic: quoting a particularly overblown sentence of Lee's, he comments 'Such a sentence pops when trodden upon, like seaweed'. Finally, although the book is clearly not worth much attention, he moves beyond it in this short review to offer reflections on the function of royalty in the modern world and on the nature of responsible biography. The life of the late king, he declares, quietly but devastatingly, is not 'of importance to the universe or even to Europe' because he lacked 'distinction of spirit'. Very characteristic, again, is this movement from the specific and the banal to fundamental moral issues, and this unshakable confidence in his own possession of the truth. Even in such a brief occasional piece, much of the essential Forster is to be found and it is not too much to say that no-one but Forster could have written it in quite that tone and those terms.

Forster's later years were outwardly uneventful, as indeed his earlier years had largely been, and an account of them can be given quite summarily. When his mother died in 1945, at the age of ninety, he was crushed by the blow, but he remained active and kept his many friendships in good working order, partly by means of a voluminous correspondence. (Since he never employed an agent but dealt with all his own business correspondence, and since his fan-mail in his later years was enormous, he was a letterwriter on the scale of the great

Victorians.) He travelled quite widely, revisiting India in 1945, America in 1947 and 1949, and the Continent for holidays even in the last decade of his life. From 1946, having lost his home with his mother's death, he resided at King's College, Cambridge, where – half a century and more after his own undergraduate years – he befriended undergraduates and became a familiar figure. He was much sought out by visitors to Cambridge, and was, in V. S. Pritchett's phrase, 'a kind of wayward holy man' and, as Furbank notes, 'an object of pilgrimage, particularly for visiting Indians'.[20] Forster himself wryly noted that 'Being an important person is a full time job',[21] but his fame went beyond that of a writer whose books had become classics in his lifetime. Not only was he, on account of his great age, a survivor from a vanished late-Victorian and Edwardian period that people were beginning to take more and more seriously, but he was venerated as a sage or guru whose convictions, tirelessly enunciated over a long lifetime, were seen as acutely relevant to the nuclear age. When, for example, in a 1957 interview he told Angus Wilson that the world was divided into sheep and goats, and that the goats were marked by a 'failure to love',[22] this was no more than he had been saying in one way and another for more than half a century, but it was also recognised as relevant to a world of embattled superpowers. Not just fame but wisdom and even a kind of 'holiness'[23] (Furbank's word) were part of the Forsterian charisma. Furbank sums up the matter well when he says that the last twenty years of Forster's life were 'a period of idolization. He had come to be honoured for personal goodness and sanctity, to an extent that perhaps few writers have known'.[24]

More superficial kinds of honour were not absent. He declined a knighthood, but accepted the award of higher distinctions, that of a Companion of Honour in 1953 and in 1969 the Order of Merit. Quite late in his life he found a new outlet for his literary activities, and a way of putting his writing to the service of his lifelong love of music, by producing in 1951, with the collaboration of Eric Crozier, a libretto for Benjamin Britten's opera *Billy Budd*, based on Melville's story. A less public kind of literary activity was a return to the short story, with which he had begun his career as a writer so long ago: 'The Other Boat', perhaps the finest short story he ever wrote, was produced in 1957–8, when he was nearly eighty, though it

was not published until it appeared, along with other stories
unpublished during his lifetime, in the posthumous volume *The
Life to Come* (1972). As we have already seen, he also took up
Maurice once again at about this time.

Forster died on 7 June 1970, in Coventry, at the home of
close friends of long standing. Friends had always been of
central importance in his life: for him, friendship was not one of
the minor amenities of civilised existence but something to be
taken with the utmost seriousness, worked at, kept in good
repair, and valued intensely and passionately. For Forster, the
agnostic bachelor, his friends had the kind of importance that
for many men belongs to their wives, their children, or their
God. Though he was only a peripheral member of the
Bloomsbury Group (he told K. W. Gransden that he did not
regard himself 'as belonging or having belonged to Bloomsbury'),
he shared their cult of personal relationships, and it is an
attitude that permeates almost everything he wrote, fiction and
non-fiction alike. Bloomsbury was, of course, very much a
product of Cambridge, and it was at King's in around 1900
that Forster had been converted, once and for all, to a belief in
friendship that J. R. Ackerley, in the passage already quoted,
describes as 'almost mystical'.

In his biography of his Cambridge mentor G. L. Dickinson,
Forster describes Dickinson's reactions to his visits to America
and China. In the United States, Dickinson found 'So much
cordiality, so little intimacy, such gleaming teeth, so little
tenderness, so little fusion!' whereas in China, 'They understood
personal relationships in the sense in which he and Cambridge
understood them and America has failed to understand them'.[25]
Whether these observations are just is less important than the
light they throw on Dickinson's attitudes and his influence on
Forster: societies are tested by their capacity for 'intimacy' and
'tenderness' and their understanding of 'personal relationships'.
Forster develops the point in one of his best-known essays,
'What I Believe,' included in *Two Cheers for Democracy*. This
personal creed begins, as one might have guessed, with 'personal
relationships', of which he writes that they

> are despised today. They are regarded as bourgeois luxuries,
> as products of a time of fair weather which is now past, and
> we are urged to get rid of them, and to dedicate ourselves to

some movement or cause instead. I hate the idea of causes, and if I had to choose between betraying my country and betraying my friend, I hope I should have the guts to betray my country.

The date of the essay is 1939, which gives point to the reference to dedication 'to some movement or cause', the 1930s in England having been dominated by the dazzling talent of W. H. Auden, a fully, indeed multifariously, 'committed' writer. It also brings home the courageous unconventionality of the second sentence quoted.

Subsequently, however, and even since Forster's death, the reference to 'betraying my country' as the possible price of loyalty to an inner circle of friends has acquired an ominous and quite unforeseen significance in the light of what we now know about the Cambridge-educated spies of the interwar generation. Perhaps this is one of the reasons why Forster's reputation as a sage has been on the decline since his death. It is, though, a perfectly familiar phenomenon for a writer who has enjoyed a great following in his lifetime to suffer a posthumous decline in esteem; and it is probably too early to say whether the trend will in due course be reversed, as has so often happened in other cases. In any case we ought to distinguish between Forster's status as a public figure or guru – that is, the veneration and trust that were felt for him as a guide to thinking on ethical, social and political issues – and his permanent status as a writer. Our concern in this book will be primarily with his achievement as a novelist, and with those aspects of his work that may be regarded as of enduring value and interest.

2

The Italian Novels

Where Angels Fear to Tread (1905)

A Room with a View (1908)

The first and third of the five novels that Forster published during his lifetime are customarily referred to as his 'Italian novels'; it is reasonable to group them together since they not only both make use of Italian settings but derive from the same experiences, were begun at about the same time, and share certain qualities of theme, characterisation and tone. The prolonged visit to Italy on which Forster and his mother embarked in the autumn of 1901 has been described as 'the most fruitful journey of his life', since 'out of it sprang his earliest stories and two of his first three novels'; Forster himself said that the 'creative element' had been 'freed' by his encounter with Italy.[26] What he had been freed from – in spirit if not in body – were the constraints and inhibitions imposed by English middle-class society, with its indifference to art, its suspicion of pleasure, its cramping notions of 'good form' and its rigid class barriers; what Cambridge had begun, Italy completed. In his first published novel, Sawston (usually regarded as a portrait of Tonbridge, where he and his mother lived during his schooldays) is the negative side of the picture, as Italy is the positive.

According to Forster's own account the germ of *Where Angels Fear to Tread* was a snippet of conversation, overheard in a hotel lounge during the Italian visit, in which one English lady was telling another about 'a third English lady who had married an Italian far beneath her socially and also much younger, and how most unfortunate it was'.[27] Here, in the idea of a marriage that unites the two different cultures, and the judgment by others that it was to be deplored on social and other grounds, is the essence of what was to become a polished and skilfully-constructed novel. However, Forster does not seem to have been in a hurry to make use of this suggestive bit of eavesdropping: as so often with the raw material that writers accumulate by chance, it seems to have needed to ripen in his mind before he was ready to take it up. When he returned from Italy, he produced essays and short stories and began work on a novel called *Lucy* that turned out to be an early version of *A Room with a View*. At some point, though, he began another Italian novel – during 1904 he worked on both of them – but as they progressed the second one evidently seized his interest more firmly, for at the beginning of December 1904 he notes that the 'Lucy novel' has been 'laid aside for a bit', having got as far as Chapter 9, and the other novel – at this stage tentatively titled *Rescue* – is near completion.[28] By the end of the year it was finished except for revisions; these apparently did not take long, for by the following spring it had been submitted to, and accepted by, the old-established firm of Blackwood. By this time the title had been changed to *Monteriano* but the publishers, taking the view that this was not arresting enough to attract buyers, asked Forster to think again. The final title was suggested by his Cambridge friend E. J. Dent, and the novel was published in October 1905.

Where Angels Fear to Tread uses two contrasted settings: a small town in the Home Counties called Sawston, and a small town in Tuscany called Monteriano (apparently based on San Gimigniano). They are connected by the translation of four of the English characters to the Italian setting; to effect this three journeys to Italy are made, for a variety of reasons, in the course of the story. At the beginning Lilia, a widow of thirty-three, accompanied by Miss Caroline Abbott, who is twenty-three, sets off (as Forster had done) for a prolonged sojourn in Italy as a tourist. When news reaches Lilia's in-laws in Sawston that she intends to marry an Italian, her brother-in-law Philip Herriton is dispatched post-haste to bring her to her senses; but he arrives too late, and he returns home, accompanied by Caroline, having failed in his mission. This is the first of two rescue parties, and it exemplifies, at this stage superficially and ironically, the idea of being 'saved' – one of the central concepts in Forster's work. Later, when Lilia dies giving birth to a child, Philip is sent out again, this time in the unattractive company of his sister Harriet, to 'rescue' the Anglo-Italian baby so that it may be taken back to Sawston and receive the advantages of an English middle-class Protestant education. This time, unknown to the others, Caroline makes her own way to Monteriano; thus this rescue operation is more complex than the previous one. It is also more tragic in its results, since the baby, which was to have been 'saved' from its Italian father and Catholic upbringing, is killed in an accident after Harriet has stolen it from its father.

So much for the outlines of the story, and it will be seen at once that in this very short novel Forster has contrived to touch on most of the major events of life and the major themes of fiction: love and marriage, birth and death. Until the last twenty pages, the tone is predominantly light, even comic, in the vein of social and domestic comedy that has a long tradition in the nineteenth-century English novel and that Forster seems to have learned from his reading of Jane Austen (for whom he had a particular admiration), Meredith and others. In the closing pages of the novel the tone changes almost abruptly, and we are given high drama (or melodrama), including a kidnapping, a mysterious stranger, a madcap flight, sudden death, physical violence, attempted murder, and (for once) a successful rescue in the nick of time. To say all this, however, is to consider only the surface of the novel – though the surface undeniably possesses its own importance and effectiveness.

For the central concern of the story is not with outward events but with inner lives, especially those of Philip and Caroline. In the previous chapter I quoted Forster's remark that the world was divided into sheep and goats, those who are capable or incapable of love, and the characters in his novels are also often aligned in this way. The arrogant, power-hungry and convention-bound matriarch Mrs Herriton and her bad-tempered, censorious Low Church daughter Harriet, are unmistakably of the latter class; but Philip and Caroline learn that life is greater than they had imagined. In other words, they transcend their emotional and spiritual conditioning and by the end of the novel have changed, profoundly and permanently. Many readers, nearing the end of the novel for the first time, naturally assume that a happy ending is in store, with a marriage of true minds promised for a newly enlightened Philip and Caroline. Forster does not give us this ending, for by this

not at all clear who is to be the central figure in the story. Lilia is the centre of attention at the station, with Caroline hovering quietly in the background ('conducting her adieus in a more decorous manner on the platform'). Lilia, as a widow, is ostensibly going to Italy as Caroline's chaperone; but it soon becomes clear that the real situation is the reverse, with the younger and unmarried Caroline keeping an anxious eye on the flighty behaviour of the irresponsible Lilia. With Lilia's marriage and the failure of the first rescue party, followed by the account of her marital unhappiness, she does seem temporarily to occupy the centre of the stage and the reader might be forgiven for supposing that she is to be the heroine of the novel, especially since she becomes the only one of the English characters left behind in Italy.

But Lilia is not the stuff of which heroines are made, at least in a novel by E. M. Forster, for although her disillusion and unhappiness are perfectly genuine and even touching, she acts almost entirely on impulse and has no more moral life than a domestic pet. In any case, she dies when the novel is only about one-third through, and the question again arises, who is to provide the central interest.

This time it is not so readily answered, but as we read on we become aware that the role is shared by Philip and Caroline, and that the relationship between them, which grows slowly and of which neither of them is really aware, is also significant. Both are, of course, products of Sawston. Being a man, Philip has partially escaped from its constraints and works as a barrister in London (not very successfully, it appears). He has the reputation of being clever and unconventional, but in reality is without deep feelings or convictions: Forster's word for him is 'trivial', and his famous phrase 'the undeveloped heart' (see p. 4 above) is also applicable to Philip. As for Caroline, she looks after her widowed father, goes to church and engages in good works: although not at all unattractive (at the beginning of the novel she is described as 'tall' and 'rather nice-looking'), she seems set on a course leading to a life of narrow spinsterhood.

Both of them are radically changed by their experiences. The possibility of salvation that exists within Caroline is suggested as early as Chapter 5, where she and Philip have a conversation about Sawston. Perhaps significantly, the dialogue takes place on a train when they are travelling from Sawston to Charing

Cross; and it gives Philip, who is rather routinely cynical about
Sawston values, the first hint that Caroline feels strongly on
the subject and that there may be more to her than he has
suspected:

> 'I hated Sawston, you see.'
> He was delighted. 'So did and do I. That's splendid. Go on.'
>   'I hated the idleness, the stupidity, the respectability, the
> petty unselfishness.'
>   'Petty selfishness,' he corrected. Sawston psychology had
> long been his speciality.
>   'Petty unselfishness,' she repeated. 'I had got an idea that
> everyone here spent their lives in making little sacrifices for
> objects they didn't care for, to please people they didn't love;
> that they never learned to be sincere – and, what's as bad,
> never learned how to enjoy themselves. That's what I
> thought – what I thought at Monteriano.'

It is quite clear that, although she has been less vocal on the
subject, Caroline's understanding of the unsoundness of Sawston
values is profounder than Philip's, and the insight has come to
her through the contrast provided by Italy.

In the same conversation she defends Lilia's marriage, which
Sawston has greeted only with outrage:

> If they wanted to marry, why shouldn't they do so? Why
> shouldn't she break with the deadening life where she had
> got into a groove, and would go on in it, getting more and
> more – worse than unhappy – apathetic till she died?

'Apathetic' is a key-word: for Forster, unhappiness is a lesser
evil than the loss of capacity to feel. The whole dialogue is
subtle and important, and Caroline emerges in it for the first
time as a potential heroine, with an inner life and a character
very human in its inconsistencies. No wonder Philip feels a
little put out: 'For a moment Miss Abbott had seemed to him
more unconventional than himself.'

The turning-point of the novel comes almost exactly halfway
through, when Caroline has a crisis of conscience concerning
the baby and, in defiance of social tact, asks the Herritons what
they propose to do about it. Philip is blind to the moral aspect

of the case and reacts very conventionally, seeing her behaviour as 'colossal impertinence', but for Caroline it is a moral issue in which she is directly concerned, since 'The child came into the world through my negligence . . . . It is natural I should take an interest in it.' This leads Mrs Herriton to a very characteristic action: she develops a sudden interest in the baby's welfare not through any genuine love or sense of duty but because she cannot bear that the initiative should come from outside the family that she rules. As the narrator makes clear: 'Pride was the only solid element in her disposition. She could not bear to seem less charitable than others.' What counts, Forster seems to be saying, is not action but motives; whereas both women are impelled to the same line of conduct, Caroline is moved by an ideal and a genuine moral sense, Mrs Herriton only by her concern for public opinion. From this scene follows everything that happens in the rest of the novel, for Caroline's moral zeal will not permit her to accept – as the Herritons would be only too happy to do – that enough has been done when Gino has refused the offer that they should bring up the baby. Chapter 5 ends with Mrs Herriton 'looking out the trains', and three of the Sawston characters are again transplanted to Monteriano.

It is worth asking why Forster sends Harriet to Italy, and the answer must be that her refusal to change throws into relief the changes that take place in Philip and Caroline. Harriet's religion is of a gloomy and life-denying variety, and has the effect of making her censorious and irritable: when Philip comes across her prayer-book, it is open at the grim text, 'Blessed be the Lord my God, who teacheth my hands to war, and my fingers to fight', and when she holds the baby she is compared to 'some bony prophetess – Judith, or Deborah, or Jael'. (This second quotation is a good example of Forster's economical use of detail that is not merely local or arbitrary but suggestive and proleptic; Judith and Jael both committed murder, and Harriet's action brings about the death of the child.) Harriet stands for a strict uncompromising morality that attaches more importance to rightness than to love, and in this respect she is a worthy representative of Sawston, where outward forms and observances count for more than the inner spirit. The strongest possible contrast with such an attitude to life comes when Caroline watches Gino bathing his son and she experiences a kind of enlightenment or conversion:

The horrible truth, that wicked people are capable of love, stood naked before her, and her mortal being was abashed. . . the comfortable sense of virtue left her. She was in the presence of something greater than right or wrong.

Sawston prides itself on a confident, unshakable knowledge of 'right and wrong', but at this moment Caroline breaks free from its restraints and becomes a new woman.

Forster also makes Caroline realise, however, that the problem is a complex one: it would be much simpler if Sawston could be identified with everything that is deplorable and Italy with everything that is desirable, but this kind of simplification would be an untruthful account of how things stand. Sawston possesses qualities that ought not to be despised – efficiency, for instance, and order, and cleanliness – whereas Italy is beset by incompetence and corruption. (Forster later makes a somewhat similar point in *Howards End* when he contrasts the Schlegels and the Wilcoxes.) As Caroline tells Philip in Chapter 8, the choice is not between the wholly bad and the wholly good:

> Do you want the child to stop with his father, who loves him and will bring him up badly, or do you want him to come to Sawston, where no one loves him, but where he will be brought up well?

And she tells Philip to choose 'which side you'll fight on'. To fight for what one believes in is a familiar metaphor in the Bible and in the Christian hymnody ('Fight the good fight', 'Put on the whole armour of God'), but Forster's passionate agnosticism appropriates it from his orthodox upbringing and puts it to new uses. In the same passage Caroline reproaches Philip with moral laziness: he has a good brain but 'when you see what's right you're too idle to do it'.

The effect of what I have called Caroline's conversion is that she becomes convinced that they ought not to try to take the baby away from Gino; and the religious associations of the word 'conversion' are not at all irrelevant, for the climax of this phase of her experience comes near the end of Chapter 7, when she holds the baby and, 'with twenty miles of view behind her' and Gino kneeling beside her 'with his hands clasped before him', she forms part of a group that is explicitly compared to an

Old Master painting of the Virgin and Child. Caroline originally came to Italy to look at paintings; now she seems to have entered into one, and she is never the same again.

Two other episodes in the latter part of the novel call for special mention. They are both presented in dramatic terms, though one is richly comic and the other near-tragic. The first, the visit to the opera near the end of Chapter 6, is a practical demonstration of the social virtues of the Italian temperament: relaxed, uninhibited, gregarious, the audience at the third-rate production of *Lucia di Lammermoor* do not approach great art solemnly but in the expectation of its giving pleasure. (Forster had attended a performance of Donizetti's opera in Florence in 1903.) Harriet, on the other hand, is summed up in a single sentence: 'though she did not care for music, [she] knew how to listen to it', and she firmly rebukes the Italian audience who are venturing to express only their delight in the music. When Philip sees Gino and his friends and is hauled up, 'swinging by his arms', into their box, he symbolically changes sides, rejecting the frigid propriety of Harriet in favour of the warmth and enthusiasm of Gino's party and the spontaneous intimacy of a 'light caress of the arm across his back'.

These references to arms are taken up later when Philip's arm is broken in the accident that kills the child. (Forster had broken his right arm on the steps of St Peter's, Rome, in February 1902.) A little earlier in Chapter 8, as already noted, the tone has changed; the change occurs quite suddenly when a note from Harriet is brought to Philip by the local idiot, dumb and 'ghastly' in appearance, who later turns out to have been Harriet's accomplice in the theft of the baby. In the next chapter Philip goes to see Gino and there occurs one of the strangest scenes in all Forster's fiction. Philip assumes the blame for what has happened – a little quixotically, since Harriet certainly ought to bear a part of it – and tells Gino: 'It is through me. . . . It happened because I was cowardly and idle. I have come to know what you will do.' What Gino does is to fight with him in the dark, to torture him by wrenching his broken arm, and to try to kill him. Whether such behaviour on Gino's part is psychologically plausible is open to question; but the real meaning of the scene is on a deeper level. Philip clearly wants to make an act of atonement and is prepared to suffer and if necessary die in the process, though he remains his old self to the extent of demanding that, if he is to be murdered, the job should at least be done according to the rules of fair play: 'You brute!' exclaimed the Englishman. 'Kill me if you like! But just you leave my broken arm alone.' Regarded in isolation, this specimen of the public-school code could have come from a yarn by G. A. Henty or John Buchan, and one might suspect a lapse of tact on Forster's part were it not that his phrase 'the Englishman' seems to indicate that he knew what he was doing.

The episode has been compared to that contained in the chapter titled 'Gladiatorial' in D. H. Lawrence's *Women in Love* (1921), in which Rupert Birkin fights with Gerald Crich; there is an element of sexuality in both scenes, though it is less explicit in Forster and there is evidence that he himself did not become aware of it until long after the book had been written. A sense of brotherhood is one of the effects produced by Philip's ordeal, which has also enlarged his experience beyond its former boundaries by giving him an insight into great pain, great fear and the sense of impending extinction, as well as of close physical contact. But the appearance of Caroline Abbott as a *dea ex machina* (to Philip she seems, a little later, 'like a goddess') leads to the real climax of this crucial scene, which occurs when Philip sees Caroline comforting Gino: to Philip, moved by her evident nobility of character, she seems more than human, her eyes 'full of infinite pity and full of majesty, as if they discerned the boundaries of sorrow, and saw unimaginable tracts beyond'. There follows the significant comment, 'Such eyes he had seen in great pictures but never in a mortal', which seems to echo the earlier scene in which Caroline was compared to the Virgin with Child. From being a rather heartless and conventional aesthete, Philip has undergone conversion to one for whom humanity and human values are central – and Forster does indeed use the word 'conversion' a few lines later: 'He was happy; he was assured that there was greatness in the world. . . . Quietly, without hysterical prayers or banging of drums, he underwent conversion. He was saved.' There follows the sharing between Philip and Gino of the milk that has been brought for the dead baby: a symbolic and sacramental act that brings the chapter to a conclusion of great tenderness and quiet power.

This is not quite the end of the novel which, as Lionel Trilling says, begins in 'a comedy of manners', turns into 'fierceness and melodrama' and ends in 'an enlightened despair'.[29] Philip, for whom Caroline has become 'transfigured', realises that he loves her, and then learns that she is deeply and hopelessly in love with Gino. The possibility of a conventionally happy ending evaporates; but then Forster, who was sceptical about marriage as an institution, would in any case not necessarily have regarded wedding bells as promising happiness, and a more important conclusion has been reached, though it is to be found in inner states rather than external social action. As we are told on the last page of the novel, 'all the wonderful things had happened': Caroline and Philip have had a vision of glory, a new awareness of the possibilities held out by life and the greatness of which human beings are capable, and even though they return to Sawston and their future lives may be dim and uneventful, they will never be the same again. They belong to the 'saved' just as surely as Harriet and Mrs Herriton belong to the benighted.

Many of the terms that have been used in discussing this novel, or have been quoted from it, have religious connotations: 'atonement', 'conversion', 'saved', and we recall that Forster had a pious upbringing and was descended on his mother's side from a family, the Thorntons, who were prominent members of the Evangelical group known as the 'Clapham Sect'. For all his agnosticism, Forster never discarded the characteristically Christian and even Evangelical attitude that life is, in the smallest as well as the largest ways, a moral affair. As Caroline tells Philip when she is trying to persuade him not to interfere with Gino's relationship with his son:

> Every little trifle, for some reason, does seem incalculably important today, and when you say of a thing that 'nothing hangs on it' it sounds like blasphemy. There's never any knowing . . . which of our actions, which of our idlenesses, won't have things hanging on it for ever.

Her words are prophetic, for the baby's death is the result of Mrs Herriton's arrogant pride and may be said to be precipitated by Philip's 'idleness' or lack of moral seriousness as well as Harriet's action.

Forster is above all a moralist, and his achievement in *Where Angels Fear to Tread* was to effect a successul integration of the 'moral' and the 'story'. F. R. Leavis has gone so far as to describe it as the best of his pre-war, that is to say his first four, novels, and John Colmer describes it as 'a beautifully composed novel' with 'an effortless symmetry and graceful proportion'.[30] To be fair to its successors, it attempts less than, for example, *The Longest Journey* or *Howards End*, and if they are more seriously flawed this is the price paid for their grander ambitions. Moreover this first novel is not flawless. The character of Gino, in particular, is made to carry a moral weight for which it does not seem wholly adequate. Gino is cheerful, lazy and selfish (Leavis calls him 'caddish and mercenary'), and his love for his son – a love that is, after all, possessive and self-centred to a large extent – does not really redeem him. The problem is that Forster seems to have wanted to create in Gino a representative of all he admired in the Italian temperament; and since this involved a reaction against his own nation and class rather than a deep understanding of Italians, the portrait is inevitably idealised. The *moyen sensuel* Gino is given a symbolic or representative significance that does not quite convince.

Another weakness is to be detected in some of Forster's moral epigrams or confident enunciations of general truths, not on the grounds that these are a throwback to the old-fashioned, pre-Jamesian novel, for a novelist is surely entitled to adopt whatever conventions may suit him, but because they sometimes fail to ring true. In Chapter 4, for instance, analysing, or rather asserting, the reason for the failure of Lilia's marriage to Gino, Forster writes:

> No one realized that more than personalities were engaged; that the struggle was national; that generations of ancestors, good, bad or indifferent, forbade the Latin man to be chivalrous to the northern woman, the northern woman to forgive the Latin man.

This is pretentious and portentous rather than persuasive and the truth is that Forster did not know very much about what makes marriages work or not work and, to conceal his ignorance, resorted to this smokescreen of cultural or ethnic generalisation. The marriage has failed because they have nothing in common: Lilia married Gino on an idle whim and a passing attraction, he married her for her money. It is absurd to suggest, as Forster in effect does, that all would have gone smoothly if Gino had permitted his wife to take solitary walks or to run a church bazaar in Monteriano. Frederick C. Crews suggests that 'the only possibility of success for the Gino-Lilia marriage would have been a mutual interest in sex',[31] but Forster was not writing at a time when this aspect of their relationship could have been explored in an English novel, nor in any case was he the writer to be able to do it.

But these are not major reservations, and Forster's first published novel remains a remarkable performance for a young writer and a minor classic in its own right. His mastery of structure, of the presentation of moral themes through a series of dramatic scenes, of dialogue and of comedy, was already considerable. More than this, his work was already markedly original (a word used by many of the reviewers of 1905), even idiosyncratic. This quality is to be seen in, for example, the tiny incident that ends the first chapter, in which Mrs Herriton finds that the sparrows have eaten the peas she has sown and that only the torn-up fragments of the letter remain in the garden. 'disfiguring the tidy ground'. The tone of the incident, never referred to again, is casual and comic but the trivial episode has the power of a poetic symbol. Mrs Herriton, seeking to impose her rigid views on the garden as well as on her family, has sown the seeds with precision in a straight line, but the forces of life have proved too strong for her, as they do in her attempt to make Lilia conform to Sawston standards of decorum and her attempt to secure possession of the baby. This blend of comedy and moral seriousness is very characteristic and we shall find it recurring, as some of the character-types also recur (for example, that of the domineering older woman), in the novels that follow.

The origins of *A Room With a View*, Forster's third published novel, go back further than those of any of his other novels. When he died in 1970, an envelope was found among his papers labelled 'Lucy stuff' and containing 117 sheets; elsewhere among his papers were other drafts and notes. These constitute the surviving fragments of two early versions, usually referred to as 'Old Lucy' and 'New Lucy', of what eventually became *A Room with a View*.[32]

The earliest notes were made at the end of 1901 or the beginning of 1902, when Forster was in Italy with his mother, and it is clear that many of his observations and reflections during that period, some of them recorded in his diary and letters, found their way into his novel. In Florence, for instance, the Forsters stayed at the Pensione Simi, which – like the Pension Bertolini in the novel – enjoyed a view of the Arno and suffered from a Cockney landlady. In a letter of 30 October 1901, Forster writes to his friend Dent that they are moving into the Pensione Simi the next day because 'my mother hankers after an Arno view and a South aspect', which were both lacking in their present pension, and on the first page of the novel the English ladies express an identical hankering. By December the Forsters had moved on to Perugia, where they found in the hotel '12 ladies . . ., mostly middle-aged and gushing' and 'one solitary man . . . who fled and was seen no more'. These tart phrases occur in a letter written by Lily; Forster himself, writing to Dickinson three months later, complained even more caustically that everything he saw in Italy had a 'horrible foreground of enthusiastic ladies'. His mother's letter also refers specifically to a Miss Emily Spender, a romantic novelist ('so gushing about nothing'), who provided the prototype for the aptly named Miss Lavish, and also to a girl chaperoned by a middle-aged spinster, who between them must have provided some hints for Lucy Honeychurch and Charlotte Bartlett (though Charlotte seems also to have been based on Emily Forster, an aunt by marriage).[33] At a time when he cost of living on the Continent was much lower than in England, genteel English ladies of limited means were in plentiful supply in the pensions of various Italian cities and many of Forster's social contacts during his year in Italy were necessarily with this uncongenial but creatively fruitful class of person.

Back in England towards the end of 1902, Forster seems to have begun work on 'Old Lucy', the first draft of a novel based on his experiences of pension life. At this stage it was a very short novel set wholly in Italy and work on it continued during the following year. Some of the proper names, including those of Lucy, Miss Bartlett, Miss Lavish and the Pension Bertolini, had been settled on as early as the first notebook entry, though the heroine's surname at this stage is Beringer. At the end of 1903 Forster began another version of the novel and this ('New Lucy') is closer to the final work in that it introduces an English setting to contrast with the Italian scenes. In other respects too this version is closer to the published novel than is 'Old Lucy'; however, Forster's intentions do not yet allow for a happy ending, since the hero is killed in an accident after he has become engaged to Lucy. (His bicycle crashes into a tree that has fallen across the road – an incident that Forster frugally uses, with modifications, in Chapter 7 of *A Room with a View*, where the carriage luckily avoids hitting a tramline support that a storm has caused to fall.)

Forster worked at 'New Lucy' during 1904 but by this time he was also occupied not only with *Where Angels Fear to Tread* but with the early stages of *The Longest Journey*; when he ran into difficulties he seems to have put the manuscript aside, not taking it up again until 1907, when the other two novels had been completed. Still it gave him difficulties: as he wrote to Robert Trevelyan on 11 June 1907, 'I have been looking at the "Lucy" novel. I don't know. It's bright and merry and I like the story. Yet I wouldn't and couldn't finish it in the same style. I'm rather depressed....'[34] Its completion presumably demanded another year's work, since it was not published until 14 October 1908.

The opening chapter of the novel is worth considering in some detail, since it not only introduces five of the main characters and sounds some of the keynotes of the story but also provides an excellent example of the way in which Forster combines a poised and assured comic art with hints of larger issues and more momentous problems that lie beyond the cosy or claustrophobic world of the pension. Comparisons with Jane Austen are almost *de rigueur* in discussions of this novel and it is true that Forster learned a great deal from her about social comedy, acid commentary and crisp natural dialogue in which characters unwittingly reveal their own limitations. But there are also elements in this chapter that Jane Austen would never have given us and that, in combination with the more traditional elements, compose an unmistakably Forsterian blend. I am thinking, for instance, of the way in which Mr Emerson first impinges on Lucy's world – his reference to 'a view' is part of a pattern of recurring appearances of this keyword, used both literally and metaphorically, throughout the novel – and the teasing question mark that briefly discomposes Miss Bartlett, whose rigid code of conduct provides firm answers to all the questions that can possibly arise in social life.

Lucy Honeychurch comes from a well-to-do, middle-class family with a home, like Forster's own, in the country but near London. Chaperoned by her cousin Charlotte (as Forster in a sense was by his mother), she is 'doing' Italy, which means conscientiously studying the guide-book (the famous Baedeker) and visiting churches and art-galleries. Like Forster, she is seeing little of Italian life at close quarters, for the Pension Bertolini is run by a Cockney, has pictures of Queen Victoria and Lord Tennyson in the dining-room, and is patronised exclusively by English visitors. The novel opens on a note of discontent, with Charlotte complaining that their rooms have no view; and a view – or, as we might put it, 'vision' – is precisely what she lacks, since her prim, prickly attitude causes her to recoil from any new experience, any encounter that might call for adjustment of her prejudices or broadening of her narrow outlook. This kind of unconscious double meaning runs throughout the opening scene, for a moment later Lucy declares that she can 'hardly believe that all kinds of other things are just outside' – a foreshadowing of the way in which the unguessed-at world is soon to force itself on her consciousness – and very shortly afterwards an unknown old man, in defiance of all the laws of propriety, breaks into their conversation with the statement, 'I have a view'. This is Mr Emerson, an unconventional man impatient of the stifling insincerities of English middle-class behaviour, and it turns out that he has views, and strong ones, as well as a view – and not only views, but a vision of what life could be like if people would only behave rationally and naturally. A little later it turns out that he is a Socialist and has brought up his son – who also has a room with a view at the pension – on progressive lines.

Within two pages we have been introduced to four of the main characters in the novel, including the hero and heroine. Again, Forster is indebted to the nineteenth-century fictional tradition running from Jane Austen to Henry James in which a young woman, naïve and inexperienced, standing on the threshold of adult life when the novel opens, is exposed to experiences that transform her understanding of the world and eventually lead her to a mature awareness of reality. Lucy is just such a heroine, artless and easily puzzled in this opening scene by undercurrents that she senses but cannot comprehend. Some of her lines are witty in an almost Wildean manner, as when she says of Mr Beebe, 'He seems to see good in every one. No one would take him for a clergyman', but the wit is quite unconscious on her part, as is Charlotte's self-revelation when she confesses to finding it 'difficult to understand people who speak the truth'. The narrator's ironic jokes are at the expense of Lucy's artlessness and ignorance:

> Taking up Baedeker's *Handbook to Northern Italy*, she committed to memory the most important dates of Florentine History. For she was determined to enjoy herself on the morrow.

She cannot, however, be blamed for these absurdly misguided efforts, for she is a product of her class and period. More importantly, even at this early stage there is a spark of protest or rebellion in her that suggests her potential for salvation. When Miss Bartlett has rather stiffly, and after a good deal of distinctly ungracious dithering, accepted the Emersons' offer to change rooms with them, Lucy wonders to herself 'whether the acceptance might not have been less delicate and more beautiful'.

Still, for the time being, she accepts Charlotte as a social and moral guide; and Charlotte has the kind of touchy concern for the conventions, however irrational, that leads her to detect impertinence and even impropriety in behaviour that is actually quite spontaneous and innocent. She is deeply shocked when George Emerson mentions casually that his father is taking a bath and she insists that, when the exchange of rooms takes place, Lucy should not occupy the one that has belonged to the young man. The kind of sexual purity that can detect the threat of indecency in these situations is a very curious phenomenon and Lucy is bewildered by the operations of this code, which seems to her as inexplicable as the rites of some savage tribe. There is a neat symbolism in the contrasting behaviour of the two women at the end of the chapter: Lucy, feeling the oppressiveness of Charlotte's attentions, 'opened the window and breathed the clean night air', while Charlotte in her own room 'fastened the window-shutters' to exclude the larger world. This short chapter is only a dozen pages long, but already the ground has been laid for a great deal that is to follow. Not only have the prevailing attitudes – those of Forster's own class – been economically but firmly indicated, but the existence of oppositions or rebellion has also made itself felt in the Emersons and even, latently, in Lucy herself.

K. W. Gransden has some suggestive comments on Forster's use of the rigid conventions of the English middle classes, no doubt all the more rigid when their representatives were abroad and thus anxious to serve as impressive advertisements for their national virtues and to demonstrate both their solidarity and their superiority to the natives. Pointing out that the strength of these behaviour-patterns before the Great War changed English society is something that Forster found very useful as a novelist, Gransden writes:

> This may even explain in part why he has given us no novel of the post-1918 English scene. He may have lost his bearings, been bewildered by the breaking-down, by common consent, of conventions which, when he was young, required so much art and individual daring to defy. It might be said that Forster even gives the conventions more weight than they need have, more even than the age demanded; the stressing of them gave him his essential framework of social comedy, as they gave Jane Austen hers, and lent greater force to the passion and radicalism of his protests.[35]

The theme of *A Room with a View* is the hard-won destruction of convention, which (in Forster's sense of the term) is by definition neither spontaneous nor sincere, by the forces of truth and naturalness.

The six chapters that follow and complete Part One of the novel present a series of episodes that dramatise Lucy's successive contacts with reality and her responses to these experiences. The title of the second chapter, 'In Santa Croce with no Baedeker', suggests in a whimsical way that Lucy will find herself deprived of the guide-book that was both a badge of the tourist and a means of coming to terms with a strange world that might otherwise prove puzzling and even intimidating: the function of the Baedeker, which serves as a symbol both comic and serious, is to deprive the unfamiliar of its capacity to surprise by providing the materials for what W. H. Auden called a rehearsed response. (Was it perhaps by a kind of Freudian slip that Forster, as his biographer tells us, kept mislaying his guide-book and Italian dictionary during his Italian tour?)

The chapter falls into two parts: first Lucy goes out with Miss Lavish; then, when the latter has deserted her, she runs into the Emersons. The affected unconventionally of Miss Lavish is contrasted with the genuine unconventionally of Mr Emerson, who is exceptional is that he tries always to see things as they are and to tell the truth. Lucy has not yet learned to diagnose Miss Lavish's synthetic enthusiasm ('A smell! a true Florentine smell!') as the sham it is: in the next chapter she describes her as 'so original'. When she is invited to join the Emersons in looking round the church, Lucy retreats into the kind of stock response that she has learned from Charlotte: she senses that there might be some indelicacy in accepting this spontaneous suggestion, and indeed she is afraid of the spontaneous and of anything that might lead her into areas of experience where the code of her class – the unwritten moral Baedeker of the English bourgeoisie – might no longer provide clear guidance ('She was again conscious of some new idea, and was not sure whither it would lead her'). Mr Emerson addresses her with quiet sincerity and even affection:

'My dear', said the old man gently, 'I think that you are repeating what you have heard older people say. You are pretending to be touchy; but you are not really. Stop being so tiresome, and tell me instead what part of the church you want to see. To take you to it will be a real pleasure.'

Lucy's response is to find this 'abominably impertinent' – this much is automatic and inevitable – but at the same time she finds she cannot 'get cross' with Mr Emerson. Her education has still a long way to go, has hardly begun, but there are promising signs of an openness to new influences.

At first sight it looks as though George Emerson is the opposite of Lucy, as free from conventional restraints as she is bound by them. But things, as often in Forster, are not as simple as that for; George, who has (as his father says) been brought up 'free from all the superstition and ignorance that lead men to hate one another in the name of God', has not turned out to be as perfectly happy as this scheme has seemed to promise: on the contrary, he seems intensely miserable. It is evident that Forster distrusts simple solutions to complex problems, and that we are likely to go wrong if we regard Mr Emerson as a model of wisdom and enlightenment. While his wish to clear human relationships of the clutter of conventions is undoubtedly admirable, there is something a little naïve and unworldly about him. His name is borrowed from the American thinker, essayist and specialist in moral uplift, Ralph Waldo Emerson, and his portrait may owe something to Edward Carpenter, humanist and advocate of the simple life, whom Forster did not meet until 1913 but whose work he was reading as early as 1907.

Chapter 3 reintroduces Mr Beebe, the clergyman whose social manners are smooth but whose attitude to women is, at a deeper level, 'somewhat chilly': at this stage we are told only that this is 'from rather profound reasons'. The next chapter is a good example of Forster's very un-Jane-Austen-like fondness for disrupting the placid surface of his novel with sudden violence. As Lucy is walking along the streets of Florence, two Italians quarrel about a debt, one stabs the other, and the dying man, blood pouring from his mouth, leans towards Lucy 'as if he had an important message for her'. The transition from slightly discontented sightseeing to bloody tragedy takes less than ten lines. A little earlier Lucy has been reflecting that 'nothing ever happens' to her: now events take place in rapid succession and Forster's narrative, miming the confusion of Lucy's thoughts and impressions, has a staccato, disjointed quality, his normally elegant sentences shattering into fragments ('How very odd! Across something. . . .'). George Emerson suddenly appears, catches her as she faints, and escorts her home: 'She had complained of dullness, and lo! one man was stabbed, and another held her in his arms.'

What the murder has accomplished is to annihilate the space that formerly existed between Lucy and George. When she first realises that he is present she sees him 'Across something'; when she regains consciousness in his arms, he 'still looked at her, but not across anything'; and when they pause on the way back to the pension, there is again a sense of closeness: 'She stopped and leant her elbows against the parapet of the embankment. He did likewise. There is at times a magic in identity of position; it is one of the things that have suggested to us eternal comradeship.' Out of sudden death a new relationship, still unrealised, has been born: this, it seems, is the dying Italian's 'important message'.

Lucy and George are to draw even closer together in Chapter 6 but before that, in Chapter 5, which offers a kind of resting-place between two episodes of sudden drama, it becomes clear that Lucy's education has already made some progress:

> Of the many things Lucy was noticing to-day, not the least remarkable was this: the ghoulish fashion in which respectable people will nibble after blood. George Emerson had kept the subject strangely pure. . . . She doubted that Miss Lavish was a great artist. She doubted that Mr Eager was as full of spirituality and culture as she had been led to suppose. They were tried by some new test, and they were found wanting.

She is seeing the familiar with new, more sceptical eyes and in her doubt lies the possibility of her salvation. Towards the end of this chapter, Forster makes it clear that it is Italy which is bringing about this education of the heart and the moral being: 'The well-known world had broken up, and there emerged Florence, a magic city where people thought and did the most extraordinary things.' But the most extraordinary thing is still to come, and when it does it constitutes a 'test' of the kind to which Forster's major characters are often subjected.

Chapter 6, the outing to Fiesole 'to see a View' (as the title tells us), begins very much in the vein of an episode in one of Jane Austen's novels such as the outing to Box Hill in *Emma*: a social occasion brings together all the major characters so far introduced. (There is even an echo of a similar incident in *Emma* when, as a result of a mix-up, Lucy finds herself in the same carriage as Mr Emerson.) But there are elements in the chapter that have no counterpart in Jane Austen's art: for instance, the whimsical references to the coach-driver and his girl-friend as Phaethon and Persephone, which is very much in the manner of the short stories in which Forster blends mythology and fantasy. Nor would Jane Austen, who had none of his tendency to idealise the lower classes, have shown Phaethon stealing a kiss from Persephone as they drive along; but the ensuing argument, in which the characters are ranged on different sides of the question whether this piece of

impudence should be allowed to pass unpunished, is entirely in
Jane Austen's vein. Mr Eager is all for taking a strong line; Mr
Emerson sticks up for the lovers; Miss Lavish feels 'bound to
support the cause of Bohemianism', not from any inner
conviction but because it suits the role she plays; Mr Beebe
tries to act as a peacemaker. Convention wins:

> 'Victory at last!' said Mr Eager. . . .
> 'It is not victory,' said Mr Emerson. 'It is defeat. You have
> parted two people who were happy.'

The little incident is proleptic, for there is to be another, more
important kiss before the chapter ends, and another couple are
to be parted.

Again, as with the stabbing incident in Florence, Forster
administers a deliberate shock to the reader, who is 'bounced'
(to employ the term used in *Aspects of the Novel*) from
commonplace life to an almost dream-like situation in which
feelings can be openly demonstrated. As in the earlier scene, it
is an Italian who is the instrument by which Lucy and George
are brought together: after asking to be directed to the two
clergymen, Lucy is led through the wood by the carriage-
driver, falls onto a terrace covered with violets, finds George
there alone, and is kissed by him. Immediately, however,
another image is superimposed on that of the two young
people, for Miss Bartlett appears on the scene, standing 'brown
against the view'. These words, with which the chapter
concludes, fall with a bleak and chilling cadence, for at this
stage in the novel Charlotte, like Mrs Herriton in *Where Angels
Fear to Tread*, is an embodiment of the world from which Lucy
has begun to show signs of breaking away – a world that
excludes all view or vision of the grandeur and passion of which
human beings are capable.

What follows is Lucy's loss of nerve and courage: faced with
the opportunity to strike a blow for 'life', she retreats into the
familiar world of convention, turning to Charlotte for comfort
and rejecting the 'view' that has been offered her: ' "Come away
from the window, dear," said Miss Bartlett. "You will be seen
from the road." Lucy obeyed. She was in her cousin's power.'
Before this the outing has ended in confusion and a sudden
thunderstorm has mirrored the social and emotional disorder.

The next morning Lucy and Charlotte leave for Rome, and their abrupt departure represents Lucy's turning her back on the chance of love and freedom that has been offered to her. She has failed the test; the opportunity may never recur (as it does not, for instance, for Mr Lucas in Forster's very fine short story 'The Road from Colonus') and at this point the outcome of the novel could be as tragic as that of *The Longest Journey* or as wistfully inconclusive as that of *Where Angels Fear to Tread*.

By the end of Part One, then, Lucy has had, and has rejected, her opportunity of embracing a different and higher kind of life – passionate rather than suspicious of feeling, spontaneous rather than conventional, full of joy rather than fear in the face of experience. These antitheses are similar to what has already been encountered in *Where Angels Fear to Tread*, where Caroline and later Philip undergo 'conversion' from one set of moral and ethical values to another; they also resemble the doctrines that were to be expounded a few years later by D. H. Lawrence in novels and stories more experimental in style and method than Forster's (though not for that reason alone necessarily more successful or estimable). Part of the blame for Lucy's retreat into the safety of the familiar world of conventions and stock responses must be laid at the door of Charlotte, to whom she has turned in her emotional bewilderment after the episode at Fiesole, for Charlotte, guardian of the proprieties that she is, has imposed on Lucy her own version of what has happened – she speaks, for instance, of George having 'insulted' Lucy. Charlotte is at length to undergo, off-stage, her own conversion, but that is still a long way off.

Part Two opens with the scene transferred abruptly to England, and with a paragraph to which the reader, trained by Forster's numerous earlier references, from the title onwards, to views and the exclusion of views, can readily attach a more than literal meaning. The word 'view' which has already been encountered repeatedly, from the first paragraph onwards, in Italian contexts, now recurs, like the repetition of a musical motif, in the description of the Honeychurch home, and the opening lines of Part Two thus echo those of Part One:

> the drawing-room curtains at Windy Corner had been pulled to meet, for the carpet was new and deserved protection from

the August sun. They were heavy curtains, reaching almost to the ground, and the light that filtered through them was subdued and varied. . . . Without was poured a sea of radiance; within, the glory, though visible, was tempered to the capacities of man.

Windy Corner, we soon learn, has a glorious view, being 'built on the range that overlooks the Sussex Weald'; but Lucy's mother and brother are sitting in semi-darkness. It is a little hard to know what to make of this: the symbolism of the excluded view and the unwelcome sunshine might lead us to believe that we are about to meet another version of the mother and son, Mrs Herriton and Philip, in the earlier novel, but as it turns out Mrs Honeychurch and Freddy are both attractive figures – he a lively medical student, she with nothing of the matriarchal dragon about her. Perhaps the only point being made is that England is not Italy; if so, the symbol is rather dubious, since in Mediterranean countries the sun is regularly excluded by curtains and blinds. There is, too, a slightly puzzling symbolism in the name of the house, but we may be intended to recall the moment in Chapter 2 when Mr Emerson has quoted from one of the poems in A. E. Housman's *A Shropshire Lad*. In its exposed situation, Windy Corner is open to the 'twelve-winded sky' in the lines quoted, and the next stanza of the poem is relevant to the novel as a whole:

> Now – for a breath I tarry
> Nor yet disperse apart –
> Take my hand quick and tell me,
> What have you in your heart.

Of such spontaneous frankness Lucy is not yet capable.

From the conversation of her mother and brother, we learn that while in Rome she has met Cecil Vyse, who has proposed to her there and subsequently, and is even now doing so for the third time. Cecil, according to Mrs Honeychurch, is 'good', 'clever', 'rich' and 'well connected'; he has 'always gone in for unconventionality' (we recall Miss Lavish), but with some inconsistency has asked the permission of Lucy's mother before proposing to her a third time. The inconsistency betrays him; moreover, as so often in Forster, the exact turn of the colloquial phrase is revealing, since 'going in for' unconventionality, as if it were fretwork, suggests affectation rather than conviction. The narrator analyses Cecil's nature in somewhat broader terms:

> Well educated, well endowed, and not deficient physically, he remained in the grip of a certain devil whom the modern world knows as self-consciousness, and whom the medieval, with dimmer vision, worshipped as asceticism.

We have already come to identify Mr Beebe, the clergyman, with a certain misogyny, perhaps unconscious; now Cecil is identified with asceticism or celibacy. Even though he is apparently in search of a wife, it is implied that he is afraid of the body – in Forster's terms, he is Gothic rather than Greek. (This formulation perhaps owes something to Matthew Arnold's antithesis of Hebraism and Hellenism in his *Culture and Anarchy*, something to Hardy's antithesis of medievalism and paganism in *Jude the Obscure*, and something again to the Hellenic fervour of Forster's mentors Wedd and Dickinson.) The rest of the novel – more than half of it – concerns Lucy's discovery of the truth about Cecil and her own liberation from fear of the physical. Though for the moment she accepts Cecil, life presents her with a second chance of salvation; after breaking off her engagement she sinks for a time into spiritual chaos and darkness, but eventually marries George Emerson.

To accomplish this, Forster resorts to plot contrivances that are not, by the strict canons of fictional realism, particularly plausible – but then his allegiance to realism had from the very beginning of his career been less than whole-hearted. He has already relied on coincidence to have George Emerson handy to catch Lucy when she swoons after the stabbing, and on a double coincidence in relation to Mr Beebe, whom Lucy has known slightly before the Italian visit and runs into in Florence, and who conveniently moves into the neighbourhood soon after her return. Now he has the Emersons also come to live nearby, so that a small community has been assembled in which the relationships of the main triangle of characters (Lucy, Cecil, George) and of several lesser characters can all be explored. Even Miss Lavish impinges briefly on the scene. In Chapter 12, Forster introduces a conversation on coincidence between George Emerson and Mr Beebe. George believes in fate, the

randomness of happenings symbolised by the 'twelve winds' of
Housman's poem (here alluded to again); Beebe, who has
earlier said that he has never heard of *A Shropshire Lad*, argues
for a rational explanation of the so-called workings of fate –
rather curiously, since as a clergyman he might be expected to
have a professional commitment to Providence.

Houses, and places in general, are always important in
Forster's novels and stories; and in some of his more fanciful
tales such as 'Other Kingdom' he uses the notion, derived from
Greek mythology, that certain places can possess a special
potency, an almost magical quality, as if presided over by
tutelary spirits or local deities. In Chapter 9, as Lucy and Cecil
are out walking, a moment occurs at which they have to choose
between two ways, the highroad and a footpath through the
woods. (Forster had already used a somewhat similar episode
in *The Longest Journey*.) Lucy's suggestion that they keep to the
road obscurely irritates Cecil, who complains that she has
'never once been with me in the fields or the wood since we
were engaged'. The ensuing dialogue is fraught with a
significance of which neither of them is fully aware: Cecil has
sensed that she seems to 'feel more at home with me in a room',
and tells her that he connects her with 'a view – a certain type
of view', to which she confesses: 'When I think of you it's
always as in a room . . . with no view'. This reminder of the
central polarity of the novel suggests that their relationship is
ill-omened and we recall that it was outdoors, in a natural
setting of great beauty, that Lucy was kissed by George.

A scene such as this is Forster's way of explicating the full
meaning of his title: the banal phrase, part of the jargon of
hoteliers, sets up a metaphorical antithesis of an enclosed space
and a broader, almost limitless prospect. There are those like
Cecil whose spirits, civilised and circumscribed, belong entirely
within rooms, and those who, like Mr Emerson, have a view or
vision of larger possibilities. Within this scheme Cecil, though
actually belonging to the first group (as Lucy has instinctively
sensed), likes to believe that he belongs to the second: ' "I'd
rather," he said reproachfully, "that you connected me with the
open air." ' Lucy has been afforded genuine glimpses of the
view, is temperamentally qualified to step outside the room, but
has not so far had the courage to do so.

In the wood they come across 'a shallow pool' which Lucy

calls 'The Sacred Lake' and in which she has once bathed, presumably in the nude, 'till I was found out by Charlotte. Then there was a row'. Again, Forster's symbolic intentions are perceptible only just below the realistic surface. Beside the pool a serio-comic incident takes place: Cecil has never yet kissed his fiancée and now self-consciously asks her permission to do so (so much for his scorn of convention). During their awkward embrace, as different as possible from the last kiss that Lucy received, which was the result of impulse rather than calculation, Cecil's 'gold pince-nez became dislodged and was flattened between them'. He cannot, it appears, see a view without artificial aid of a kind that belongs to his class and period; and here Forster, who can sometimes be over-solemn and portentous in his commentary, makes a serious point through a felicitous touch of farce.

The pool appears again in Chapter 12, where George, Freddy and Mr Beebe bathe in it. Nude bathing was, a little surprisingly, common practice among, for instance, Cambridge undergraduates in Forster's youth, and the exuberant horseplay of the scene seems a victory for spontaneity and for the paradisal state described by Mr Emerson (here bearing a strong resemblance to Walt Whitman and his English disciple Edward Carpenter) in which 'we no longer despise our bodies'. But the idyll is interrupted by the chance appearance of Lucy, her mother and Cecil and the air becomes thick with moral disapproval. What is interesting is that the conventional reaction comes not from Mrs Honeychurch, who remains good-humoured, but from Cecil. The chapter ends with a dozen lines in which the characteristic and admirable Forsterian economy combines natural and self-revealing dialogue, realistic description, poetic symbol and comment in suddenly elevated language that anticipates Lawrence in its reference to 'a call to the blood' and recalls the quasi-religious diction ('conversion', 'salvation') of *Where Angels Fear to Tread* in some of its other phrases ('Benediction', 'holiness', 'chalice'):

'Mother, do come away,' said Lucy. 'Oh, for goodness' sake, do come.'

'Hullo!' cried George, so that again the ladies stopped.

He regarded himself as dressed. Barefoot, barechested, radiant and personable against the shadowy woods, he called:

'Hullo, Miss Honeychurch! Hullo!'
'Bow, Lucy; better bow. Whoever is it? I shall bow.'
Miss Honeychurch bowed.
That evening and all that night the water ran away. On
the morrow the pool had shrunk to its old size and lost its
glory. It had been a call to the blood and to the relaxed will,
a passing benediction whose influence did not pass, a holiness,
a spell, a momentary chalice for youth.

This is, of course, Lucy's first meeting with George since the
kiss at Fiesole. Instead of responding to him with impulsive
feeling, she retreats into a maidenly primness: she is,
significantly, 'Miss Honeychurch'. As the symbolism of the
pool makes clear, another opportunity to seize a moment of
'glory' has been allowed to pass.

According to John Colmer, though the bathing-scene 'serves
its function of establishing the value of naturalness and
spontaneous joy . . . the essence of its eroticism is homosexual
. . .; and Lucy can hardly be expected to be as stimulated by
naked man as her creator'. The objection seems not entirely
fair: Forster could hardly have depicted a scene of mixed
bathing even if he had been inclined to do so and the tone of
the passage seems to me less erotic and stimulating that
schoolboyishly hearty. Still, the erotic undertone is not altogether
absent; nor is this the only place in which the physically timid
and games-hating Forster shows a fascination with uninhibited
bodily activity (compare, for instance, the short story 'Ansell').
As in the homosexual short stories (of which more will be said
in Chapter 6), there is an element of wish-fulfilment in the
scene, and Colmer is right to imply that there is something self-
indulgent and off-centre about it since, if the encounter serves
as a test for Lucy, it is a little hard to see quite what behaviour
on her part would have constituted a pass with honours. At
such points one discerns signs of the conflict in a writer who
found himself obliged to write of the relationships of men and
women when he would have preferred to explore the relationships
between men. What is latently interesting in the scene, but
never breaks the surface, is the response of Mr Beebe – not just
his outward behaviour but his inner life.

Contrivance again makes itself felt when we learn that
Charlotte has told Miss Lavish what happened between Lucy

and George at Fiesole; Miss Lavish has put the incident into a novel; Cecil, all unconscious of the landmine he is planting, happens to read aloud the very passage to Lucy and George and George is thereupon impelled to kiss Lucy again (Chapter 15 ending with his second kiss, as Chapter 6 had ended with his first). At the end of Chapter 16, Lucy abruptly breaks off her engagement to Cecil. The abruptness is, as usual, part of Forster's narrative strategy: while some novelists might have led up to the disclosure as the surprising climax of a dramatic scene between the couple, Forster presents the scene in which Lucy tells Cecil of her feelings in Chapter 17, *after* the shock has been administered to the reader by the narrator in the last five words of the previous chapter. (Forster's chapter-endings are often worth a close look, since he likes to exploit the position of emphasis that derives from coming just before a gap in the text.) Before this, George has told Lucy, with passionate eloquence, both that he loves her and that Cecil is not a man to be taken seriously. His exposure of Cecil's shallowness liberates Lucy from the conventional judgment of him that has constituted a kind of blindness: 'The scales fell from Lucy's eyes. How had she stood Cecil for a moment?' To regain her vision is to be qualified to see a view. Thus she goes halfway towards enlightenment, but instead of proceeding straight to a happy ending, with Lucy accepting and reciprocating George's love, the novel moves in an unexpected direction.

By the end of Chapter 17, having sent both Cecil and George away, Lucy tells herself that she 'could never marry': she allies herself, that is, with the asceticism, the impulse towards celibacy or denial of the body, that Mr Beebe preaches and Mr Emerson denounces. There follows one of the most central passages of direct moral comment or unblushing didacticism in all Forster's fiction: bewildered by what has happened, Lucy, in an act of unwitting symbolism, puts out the lamp and decides that

> It did not do to think, nor, for the matter of that, to feel. She gave up trying to understand herself, and joined the vast armies of the benighted, who follow neither the heart nor the brain, and march to their destiny by catchwords. The armies are full of pleasant and pious folk. But they have yielded to the only enemy that matters – the enemy within.

Forster's 'armies of the benighted' recall the 'ignorant armies' who 'clash by night' in the last line of Matthew Arnold's poem 'Dover Beach', and Lucy has failed to heed Arnold's very Forsterian injunction that hope for mankind lies in truth in personal relationships ('Ah, love, let us be true/To one another!'). Forster, however, offers nothing of Arnold's comprehensive diagnosis of social ills and loss of faith: his concern is with private lives, not public issues – with the health of the individual soul. To know thyself is the beginning of wisdom, and when Lucy gives up 'trying to understand herself' she retreats into the darkness.

Once again she has turned down a chance of fulfilment and happiness, and now seems set on a course that will in time turn her into a close copy of Charlotte – a touchy spinster, obsessed with trivialities and imaginary issues and savouring nothing of life's greatness. However, another chance presents itself, and it is quite unpredictably engineered – or at least it has not been prevented, which amounts to the same thing – by none other than Charlotte, though Forster saves the disclosure, which transforms Charlotte into a kind of heroine, until the last page of the novel and leaves her motive a matter for speculation.

Lucy unexpectedly finds herself alone with Mr Emerson, who tells her that she is 'in a muddle'. The word is a great favourite of Forster's, used by him with a weight of meaning that turns it into a personal watchword that acquires a highly individual definition through its appearance in a variety of contexts. Though nowadays used mainly in childish, petty or semi-facetious circumstances, it may once have possessed more substance: 'All a muddle!' is, for instance, the wholly serious and comprehensive indictment of the social order made by Dickens's Stephen Blackpool in *Hard Times*. By Forster it is used in all seriousness, and a sense of what he intends to convey by it can be deduced from one of Mr Emerson's speeches to Lucy:

'Take an old man's word: there's nothing worse than a muddle in all the world. It is easy to face death and Fate, and the things that sound so dreadful. It is on my muddles that I look back with horror – on the things that I might have avoided. We can help one another but little. I used to think I could teach young people the whole of life, but I

know better now, and all my teaching of George has come
down to this: beware of muddle. Do you remember, in that
church, when you pretended to be annoyed with me and
weren't? Do you remember before, when you refused the
room with the view? Those were muddles – little but
ominous – and I am fearing that you are in one now.'

Lack of truth-telling, dishonesty with oneself and in personal
relations, failure to see things as they really are, behaviour not
spontaneous but dictated by convention, and the substitution of
convenient illusion for disturbing reality: these lead to 'muddle'
and a loss of the chance of greatness of which life, for all its
flaws, is capable.

Mr Emerson proceeds to tell Lucy, with a frankness quite
uninhibited by social rules, that she loves George 'body and
soul'. He expounds the phrase to her:

'I know by experience that the poets are right: love is
eternal. . . . I only wish poets would say this too: that love is
of the body; not the body, but of the body. Ah! the misery
that would be saved if we confessed that!'

At first Lucy is conventionally angry and indignant; but she
cannot resist the truth when it is told her so plainly. She
abandons the idea of going to Greece with a pair of old maids,
and marries George. Their honeymoon is spent at the Pension
Bertolini, so that the novel ends where it has begun.

Colmer has suggested that it is 'the central weakness of the
novel that Lucy's emancipation from the spirit of muddle
should have to come from Mr Emerson . . ., when the reader
feels it should come from his son', and that George is 'too
passive' to be a satisfactory hero. This objection can perhaps be
extended into a more general complaint that the Emersons,
father and son, are too abstract in conception and are
insufficiently realised, with the result that George's behaviour
often seems unmotivated and his father no more than a
mouthpiece for Forster's sermonising. We never see George
from the inside and the probable truth is that Forster was not
really much interested in either the educational theme (George
as a failure or partial failure of his father's enlightened rationalist
system), which is perfunctorily treated, or in George's role as a
lover. It might even be argued that Forster's famous abruptness,

for instance in the scene at Fiesole, is an attempt to bluff the reader into accepting as natural what is never plausibly accounted for in psychological terms.

As for Mr Emerson, Forster undoubtedly sympathised with, and may have envied, the radical outlook that he represents; but his own life was not at this time notable for its unconventionality, and it is doubtful whether he really understood what it was like not merely to hold but to act on opinions that flew in the face of middle-class notions. Mr Emerson has a weakness similar to that of Gino in the earlier novel: he serves as an antithesis to the attitudes that Forster wanted to expose as hollow and false and as an embodiment of what is to be admired and emulated, but neither character is quite substantial enough, dramatically speaking, to support this role. Forster's problem was that he knew the Charlottes and the Mr Beebes of this world much more thoroughly and intimately than he knew the Mr Emersons or the Ginos. Moreover, as F. R. Leavis has pointed out, one has 'to question the substantiality of the wisdom that Mr Emerson seems intended to represent': his doctrines are clearly a good thing but are never defined with much exactness, and the final impression of this character is less of wisdom than of well-meaning but largely ineffectual eccentricity.

These weaknesses apart, the novel has a remarkable moral and technical assurance, retains its freshness after some eighty years, and bears repeated re-readings. In Jane Austen, Forster had found not only a model for witty and revealing dialogue and the development of a theme through a series of small-scale encounters and social occasions (he learned from her, as he said in a 1952 interview, 'the possibilities of domestic humour'), but also an exemplar of the virtues of economy and strict relevance in a work of fiction. The expansiveness of the Victorian novel, with its rendering of extensive tracts of time – a tradition still alive in, for instance, such Edwardian novels as Arnold Bennett's *The Old Wives' Tale* (1908) – has been displaced in Forster's 'Italian' novels by a much terser mode of writing in which many of the most telling effects are created by the epigram, the brief moral generalisation, the revealing inflection or idiom in dialogue, the recurring key-word, and the use of parallels, cross-references and poetic symbols to create what Forster later referred to as 'rhythm' in the novel – a quality that we shall have occasion to refer to again.

3

The Longest Journey

The Longest Journey (1907) seems to have been Forster's favourite among his novels, perhaps for the same reason that made Dickens regard *David Copperfield* as his 'favourite child': there is in it a strong element of autobiography and in particular some resemblance between the hero and the author, though this is an element that ought not to be exaggerated. Rickie Elliot is an orphan who has been unhappy at school but finds happiness at Cambridge; he has a small private income; he is physically weak and has been lame since birth; and he writes stories that introduce Greek mythology into modern settings, 'pretending that Greek gods were alive, or that young ladies could vanish into trees' (Ch. 16). Much of this was, in one way or another, true of Forster himself, the lameness perhaps symbolising his homosexuality. Although in many respects naïve and immature, Rickie is capable of speaking with passionate conviction and moral force – another characteristic shared with his creator. At the same time, Rickie is easily influenced; he joins, at any rate temporarily, the 'armies of the benighted' and his life ends prematurely in failure and futility; though this may express some of Forster's fears and doubts about his own nature, it can hardly have represented his considered assessment of his own nature and potentialities.

Forster's partiality for the novel is, then, easy to understand; but few of his critics have awarded it the prize over all the other novels, though most have been ready to recognise that it aspires to a greater seriousness and a more ambitious scope than the 'Italian' novels that immediately preceded and followed it. Pointing out that it is the first of three 'English' novels (the others being *Howards End* and *Maurice*), Colmer states that the theme of all three is 'England, the continuity of the English tradition, the question of who shall inherit England', and also

51

notes an interesting similarity in the pastoral coda with which each of the three novels concludes. For Gransden it is 'the most romantic and passionate of the novels' and is central to Forster's work: 'no one can simultaneously dislike it and care for Forster as a writer'. Trilling regards it as 'perhaps the most brilliant, the most dramatic and the most passionate of his works', while noting at the same time that it is also 'by conventional notions the least perfect – the least compact the least precisely formed' (Trilling had not read *Maurice* at this time). Rex Warner echoes Trilling's view in finding it 'strangely moving and revealing' at the same time that it contains 'more faults than any other which Forster wrote'. W. J. Harvey judges it 'a failure' and attributes its failure to the fact that Forster's 'ambition has outrun his technical resources' and that 'The moral emphasis and the dramatic power of the book not only do not coincide; they are in direct conflict with each other'. For Furbank it is a 'queer, ardent, fumbling affair'. Forster himself said, with some exaggeration, that 'it is a novel which most readers have dismissed as a failure'.[36] As these quotations suggest, there is no consensus concerning Forster's second-published novel: the most widely held view is that it tackles large themes but that the treatment is not wholly adequate to the subject.

The Longest Journey was published on 16 April 1907, but its origins go back several years, and a number of elements in the novel have been shown to be based on personal experience. The first section draws on Forster's undergraduate years and his subsequent visits to Cambridge, and the opening chapter specifically recalls the Saturday evening meetings of 'the Apostles': the lines from Shelley's *Epipsychidion* that provide the novel's title had been quoted by J. T. Sheppard at an Apostles' meeting in 1903. The 'secluded dell' that Rickie visits on a walk in Chapter 2 is based on a chalk pit 'up the Madingley Road', just outside Cambridge, referred to in Forster's diary for May 1898. By the author's own account, Mrs Failing owes something to his domineering uncle, William Forster, and her country house, Cadover, is modelled on Uncle William's Northumberland home which Forster visited for holidays. (Furbank suggests, however, that this character may also be 'drawn in part' from Elizabeth von Arnim, the English wife of a Prussian count who had briefly employed Forster as a tutor.) The schoolmaster Mr Jackson is based on Isaac Smedley, who had taught Forster at

Tonbridge. Ansell may be a blend of two Cambridge friends, H. O. Meredith and A. R. Ainsworth: Lytton Strachey recognised something of Meredith in the portrait and Furbank's view is that, while Ansell's externals recall Ainsworth, his 'role as Rickie's conscience' suggests Meredith.[37]

Most important of all, perhaps, was a chance encounter with a club-footed young shepherd at Figsbury Rings, an Iron Age earthworks near Salisbury in Wiltshire, that took place on 9 September 1904. Furbank narrates this undramatic but momentous episode as follows:

> The boy was friendly, did not call him 'sir', and offered him a smoke of his pipe; and when Forster offered him sixpence as they were parting, he refused it. This apparently trivial incident took on peculiar significance for Forster. He decided that the boy was one of the most remarkable human beings he had ever met. 'What strikes me even more than his offering me his pipe to smoke is his enormous wisdom,' he wrote in his diary.[38] (pp. 116–17)

Many years later he saw the shepherd again but, as he then wrote, 'I did not speak to him nor hand over his share in the royalties of The Longest Journey'[39]

The original meeting seems to have constituted what he refers to in the novel as a 'symbolic moment': it made a deep and lasting impression and formed the basis of the third part of the novel and the character of Stephen Wonham. In the fictional account the shepherd boy was, in physical terms, idealised, his club foot being transferred to Rickie.

A couple of months earlier, on 18 July 1904, Forster had had an idea for a story about 'a man who discovers that he has an illegitimate brother' (the phrase occurs in the introduction he wrote for an edition of the novel in 1960). Conceivably the attractive figure of the Wiltshire shepherd and the brief unforced camaraderie that sprang up between them made him appear to Forster at some level of awareness as an embodiment of the brother, the ideal male companion connected by ties of blood, whom he had never known. The experience may have converged in Forster's mind with his recollection of a book he had fairly recently read, Samuel Butler's *Erewhon Revisited* (1901), in which the narrator, like Rickie Elliot, discovers that he has an illegitimate half-brother; Butler's work in general was an important influence on Forster, as he himself was ready to acknowledge.

Place is important in all Forster's novels and the three parts of *The Longest Journey* each have a place-name as title: 'Cambridge', 'Sawston', 'Wiltshire'. Of these the middle one is fictitious. Sawston, which had already appeared in *Where Angels Fear to Tread*, is a middle-class residential community near London with a minor public school that accepts day-boys – in all these respects resembling Tonbridge. In Chapter 17 we are told that Rickie was 'sensitive to places' and 'would compare Cambridge with Sawston, and either with a third type of existence, to which, for want of a better name, he gave the name of "Wiltshire"'. The novel itself implicitly makes these comparisons and they are fundamental to its moral pattern.

The first of the three parts, 'Cambridge', occupies almost exactly half the novel. It begins with a scene in which a group of undergraduates are discussing the time-honoured philosophical problem of the nature of reality: does a cow in a field continue to exist when no-one is there to look at it? S. P. Rosenbaum has argued that the discussion is 'a fairly direct allusion' to a paper titled 'The Refutation of Idealism' by the Cambridge philosopher G. E. Moore, published in the journal *Mind* – the same journal that, in the novel, publishes a criticism of Ansell's philosophical ideas – in October 1903.[40]. The discussion is dominated by Stewart Ansell, who is named first; the meeting is being held in Rickie Elliot's rooms, but Rickie's part in the argument is limited and it soon becomes clear that he is intellectually inferior to Ansell. When he tries to think about the problem in abstract terms, 'gross and senseless details' intervene, and he imagines a world full of actual cows: 'The darkness of Europe was dotted with them, and in the far East their flanks were shining in the rising sun.' (Compare Forster's own confession, in a letter of 28 October 1905: 'though "clever" I have a small and cloudy brain, and cannot clear it by talking or reading philosophy'.[41]) Rickie's imagination, and his tendency to idealise rather than to see things as they really are, are major concerns of the novel, which Gransden has gone so far as to describe as 'a meditation on the dangers and attractions of romanticism' (p. 50). At the outset it is plain that Ansell's standpoint and temperament are very different from those of his friend, and it emerges that his social background is also different, for he is the son of a provincial draper whereas Rickie's father was a London barrister. (An account of Rickie's early life is introduced, with a curious and characteristic mixture of awkwardness and audacity, in the second chapter.) This opening scene strikes a note that is to be heard repeatedly in the novel. As Trilling has said:

> The scene, delightful but apparently trivial, is a statement of what the story is about: it is about reality – appearance and reality – and the word 'real' recurs again and again in the novel.[42]

The masculine atmosphere of easy intimacy and intellectual candour is abruptly dispelled by the arrival of Agnes Pembroke, a 'tall young woman' who is visiting Cambridge with her brother as Rickie's guest but whose arrival has, no doubt revealingly, slipped his mind. Agnes's brother, Herbert, is a priggish and ambitious schoolmaster, and she is engaged to Gerald, a handsome young man who has been at school with Rickie and, as Rickie recalls only too vividly, has systematically bullied him; all three represent the world of Sawston. Agnes's arrival breaks up the discussion and Rickie's friends melt away. The most significant moment in the scene occurs when Ansell, introduced to Agnes, declines to shake her extended hand or, indeed, to recognise her existence in any way: for Ansell, it seems, she is simply not a real person and already (we are barely half-a-dozen pages into the book) Forster is engaged in his favourite strategy of aligning his characters not primarily according to social status or personal or family relationships but according to their moral worth. On the one hand is Cambridge, and its representative the clever if unconventional scholarship boy Ansell, committed to truth-telling even if it involves defying accepted codes of polite behaviour; on the other hand is Sawston, with its conventional values – values, that is, accepted not from conviction but according to notions of 'good form' – represented by the bright but empty chatter of Agnes. Rickie hovers uncertainly between the two, and this is to be his predicament for much of the novel.

In other ways, too, the scene foreshadows a great deal that follows, including the climactic confrontation near the end of

the novel between Ansell and Sawston. As Forster put it in the
introduction already referred to,

> Ansell is the undergraduate high-priest of that local shrine
> [Cambridge], Agnes Pembroke is its deadly debunker.
> Captured by her and by Sawston, Rickie goes to pieces, and
> cannot even be rescued when Ansell joins up with Stephen
> and strikes.

If this sounds a little schematic, then it must be said that that
quality is often to be found in Forster's work: as W. J. Harvey
says, the opposing forces are grouped around Rickie in 'patterns
that are significantly, even suspiciously, neat'. We have already
noted similar groupings in the Italian novels, and may also
note that the idea of 'rescue' looks back to *Where Angels Fear to
Tread*; also that the hint of misogyny in having Sawston
represented at the outset by Agnes is one that will be detected
again in Forster's work.

In Chapter 3 there occurs the first of the 'symbolic moments'
that are landmarks in Rickie's imaginative and moral life.
These moments of unexpected insight may also be referred to
as 'epiphanies', the term made current by James Joyce, for an
epiphany was a 'sudden spiritual manifestation', a moment
when everyday experience seemed flooded by a sense of radiance
and deep significance. A century earlier, in the early stages of
the Romantic tradition, Wordsworth had referred to such
instants of revelation as 'spots of time'. On a visit to Sawston,
Rickie has been a little puzzled by the conduct of Agnes and
Gerald towards each other: they exchange banalities in a way
that conflicts with his romantic and somewhat literary notion of
how lovers should behave. But when he leaves their company
and then returns unexpectedly, he finds them 'locked in each
other's arms', with the face of the commonplace Agnes
transfigured ('it shone with mysterious beauty, like some star').
Rickie is filled with a sense of glory, an awareness of life's
possibilities, and Forster describes his feelings in a purple
passage replete with romantic imagery ('pinnacles of virgin
snow', 'gods of pure flame') and religious diction ('shrines',
'benediction').

For Ansell, as we have seen, Agnes simply does not exist,
which is his way of making the point that she and her kind,

who act solely according to the dictates of convention, have no individual moral natures. For Rickie, Agnes is now endowed with the attributes of a goddess or ideal lover (we remember the mythologising and idealising tendencies of the little stories he writes). Where does the reader stand? He at least has been afforded some glimpses of Agnes' inner life that have not been granted to Rickie and knows, for instance, that she has received a vicarious sadistic thrill from Gerald's revelation that he used to inflict physical torment on Rickie. It is tempting, therefore, to see Rickie's view of Agnes as mere romantic delusion, since nothing that we have seen of her qualifies her for the role he assigns her. The trouble with this view is that Forster seems to endorse Rickie's vision of Agnes as genuinely transfigured by her love for Gerald: as F. R. Leavis says in his fine essay on Forster, 'This memory of pure uncalculating passion as a kind of ultimate . . . becomes for Rickie a criterion or touch for the real, a kind of test for radical sincerity, in his questing among the automatisms, acquiescences, blurs, and blunted indifferences of everyday living.'[43] It may be that we have here a problem similar to that arising from the scene between Gino and his son in *Where Angels Fear to Tread*: there is nothing in realistic terms – in terms, that is, of character and motivation as traditionally conceived, of consistency and plausibility – that compels our acceptance of Agnes as Rickie sees her, and if his vision of what Leavis calls 'pure uncalculating passion' is to be accepted it must be in some way for which the prevailing realistic mode of the novel has not made provision.

There is a lesser but related problem in connection with Gerald, who is also seen in a light that transforms his commonplaceness. He is a perfect physical specimen, 'a young man who had the figure of a Greek athlete and the face of an English one' (Ch. 3). A couple of pages earlier, the description of the Pembrokes' house has included a reference to 'A replica of the Hermes of Praxiteles – of course only the bust' standing in the hall (Praxiteles was one of the most famous of the classical Greek sculptors, noted for the physical perfection of his figures), and this ironic allusion to suburban prudery is echoed, without irony, in the description of Gerald ('Just where he began to be beautiful the clothes started'). Like Stephen later in the book, Gerald represents a type of robust masculinity and physical attractiveness that Rickie admires and envies but can never hope to emulate; what is surprising is that Forster seems to come close to sharing Rickie's idealised view of Gerald at the same time that he shows us the latter's coarseness of nature and bluntness of moral perception. Forster was strongly if irrationally attracted by the unreflective athletic or vigorous physical life – what he calls, in his early short story 'Ansell', 'the brainless life' – and we shall encounter it again in *Maurice* and in some of the stories (Gino is, of course, another instance of the same type).

Soon after Rickie's glimpse of what he believes to be pure, unearthly passion, Gerald suddenly dies: his neck is broken in a football match, and he expires in Agnes's arms. His death, baldly announced in the four-word sentence that opens the fifth chapter, is the most famous of all Forster's unceremonious and laconic dispatchings of his characters. Early critics were quick to react to the high mortality rate in his novels, and reviewers of *The Longest Journey* in particular took exception to this feature of the novel: as the *Athenaeum* put it, 'the introduction of Death, as a factor, is too catastrophic for art; too brusquely, at least, this god descends from the machine'.[44] Yet it can be argued that the abruptness of Forster's narrative does no more than copy the abruptness of life itself, which often enough thrusts such disasters upon us without preparation or euphemism; the only accusation that can legitimately be made is that Forster overworks the device. Rickie's reaction to Gerald's death is unexpected: he rises to the occasion, assuring Agnes with eloquence that Gerald is 'in heaven' and impressing on her the need to remember that 'the greatest thing is over'.

Again he is idealising the situation: he attempts to transform Agnes into an almost mythical figure of unassuagable grief. Just as the love of these two rather dull people, whose ordinariness has been made unsparingly clear in the dialogue, has been transformed by Rickie's romantic impulses into a grand passion, the death of Gerald transforms him into the subject of a legend and the object of a cult, a Shelley or a Rupert Brooke.

At Sawston, Rickie has encountered people of his own social class but fundamentally different from himself and his Cambridge friends: snobbish and intolerant, hidebound by the conventions of the Edwardian professional middle class, they recall the Herritons in *Where Angels Fear to Tread*. They are devoid of, and distrustful or contemptuous of, imagination – a quality that Rickie for his part has to excess. In Chapter 6 he reflects that 'real things are so wonderful' and asks himself 'Who wants visions in a world that has Agnes and Gerald?' The trouble is that his Agnes and Gerald *are* visions, the products of his romantic idealism. Rickie, moreover, is one who (in T. S. Eliot's phrase) 'cannot bear very much reality', and when his visions meet the irresistible pressure of the truth they shatter at once, with painful and destructive results. (This happens in the novel when first his memory of his dead mother and then his conviction that Stephen will not drink again are shown to be based on delusion.)

From Sawston Rickie gladly escapes back to Cambridge, for which he has 'longed passionately'. Revealingly, Gerald has expressed his scorn for what he calls the 'Varsity'; for Rickie, however, Cambridge is a refuge from the aggressive, even ruthless environment of Sawston, where superficial gentility and lip-service to somewhat threadbare ideals do not conceal ambition for material success and the world's esteem; it is also a refuge from the complexities of personal relationships, including sexual relationships (the college, where Rickie 'loved his rooms better than any person', is of course exclusively masculine). Cambridge embodies the pursuit of truth for its own sake and values people for what they are (this being a particular aspect of the truth). There is no doubt some idealisation here on Forster's part, since he neither confronts the awkward question of the morality of privilege (at whose expense, ultimately, are these young men enabled to engage in the pursuit of truth?) nor gives a real cross-section of undergraduate life (those he depicts as representing 'Cambridge' strike one as the kind he would have found, and had found, personally congenial).

But there is a wistful sense of impermanence, for Rickie is not clever and cannot hope, as Ansell does, to win a fellowship and thus prolong the Cambridge idyll indefinitely. The rooms he lives in are 'the perishable home that was his for a couple of years' (we remember that he is an orphan and has no real home), and the name of his predecessor, still faintly legible 'like a grey ghost' behind his own name painted above the door, reminds him that he too will all too soon haunt Cambridge only as a ghost or an outsider: what Sawston would call 'the real world' inexorably awaits him.

By this stage in the novel, Ansell and Agnes have emerged as representing, respectively, the worlds of Cambridge and Sawston, and in Chapter 7 Rickie's feelings for the two of them are implicitly contrasted. A substantial interval has elapsed since the events narrated in the first six chapters: the action has begun in the first term of Rickie's second year at Cambridge, and now it is the final term of his fourth and last year. He and Ansell, 'lying in a meadow', are crowned with garlands of wild flowers that Rickie has made, and the scene includes one of Forster's most eloquent passages on the friendship that the garlands symbolise:

> [Rickie] was thinking of the irony of friendship – so strong it is, and so fragile. We fly together, like straws in an eddy, to part in the open stream. Nature has no use for us: she has cut her stuff differently. Dutiful sons, loving husbands, responsible fathers – these are what she wants, and if we are friends it must be in our spare time.

Rickie knows that he must soon join 'the open stream', and the role of friend will be threatened by a society intent upon self-perpetuation and based on the institution of the family.

The latter part of the same chapter shows Agnes again visiting Cambridge, where, with some unwillingness, Rickie takes her to the dell that has already been referred to in the second chapter. The relationship of this incident to the scene with Ansell is unstated but obviously important. Agnes's instant verdict on the dell is characteristically superficial ('Oh, what a jolly place!'); for Rickie it is a place of sacred and almost magical associations, connected in his mind with the stories he writes and the Greek myths he loves. The symbolism of *A Room with a View* is briefly anticipated, for it is a spot with a view. Like the scene in the other novel in which Lucy almost falls into George's arms, what follows has a poetic, almost fabular or fairy-tale quality: Agnes enters the wood alone, then calls to Rickie, and although he tries to resist he is drawn into the little wood as if by a magic spell and finds himself in her arms. (For relevant comparisons, see Forster's short story 'Other Kingdom', published in 1909, and his essay 'My Wood', included in *Abinger Harvest*.)

Again Forster has, at a moment of emotional crisis, bypassed logical or psychological explanations in favour of a quasi-allegorical treatment; and the reader may feel that there is something seriously inadequate about Agnes's motivation at this point. Why should an attractive and ambitious young man, who has been engaged to a handsome athlete, be attracted to the puny and unresponsive Rickie, even though she regards him (or claims to do so) as 'tremendously clever'? She is hardly old enough to have grown desperate for a husband at any price, and her memory of Rickie's impressive response to Gerald's death seems an insufficient motive. The real answer is that Rickie must be shown to be won over, to his own undoing, by the Sawston camp, and for this purpose must contract a relationship that involves him deeply with the Pembrokes. This does not, however, mean that Agnes's behaviour rings true: it is as if the change from realistic to poetic and fanciful modes were a kind of sleight of hand by which Forster seeks to win assent for the implausible.

Stylistically, the crisp dialogue and narrative writing of the immediately preceding passage give way to a prose that renounces explanations and analysis:

> 'Rickie!' – and it came with the tones of an angel. He drove his fingers into his ears, and invoked the name of Gerald. But there was no sign, neither angry motion in the air nor hint of January mist. June – fields of June, sky of June, songs of June. Grass of June beneath him, grass of June over the tragedy he had deemed immortal. A bird called out of the dell: 'Rickie!'
>
> A bird flew into the dell.

As in a symbolist poem, connections and causality, which are normally prime concerns of the novelist, have disappeared, and we seem to be temporarily in a world of fairy-tale or myth – the world of Rickie's short stories (and Forster's), in which nature-worship and metamorphosis are the order of the day. Such passages, however, seem to rest a little uncomfortably in the framework of a novel largely concerned with character and motive, social class and social institutions, in a contemporary setting.

What follows is – to put it a little melodramatically, but in a way that fairly represents Forster's intention – a struggle

between Ansell and Agnes for Rickie's soul. Ansell tells Rickie
that Agnes is neither serious nor truthful (Ch. 9), and tells
another Cambridge friend that 'She caught him and makes him
believe that he caught her' (Ch. 8), 'caught' seeming to recall
the bird-imagery of the passage quoted above. But Rickie is not
swayed by his friend and, in the excitement of loving and being
loved, is already beginning to adopt the values and even the
phraseology of Sawston (his remark in Chapter 8 that he must
'get my foot on the ladder' is one of Herbert's schoolmasterly
clichés).

In Chapter 10 the scene moves to Wiltshire and two new
characters are introduced, Mrs Failing and Stephen Wonham.
The former, who is Rickie's aunt, lives in a country-house
called Cadover and is the widow of a man who has something
in common with Mr Emerson in *A Room with a View*: he has
published essays on socialism, and as an MP and an enlightened
landowner has tried to translate his ideals into action. His
widow, in contrast, is selfish and profoundly indifferent to other
people. Like Mrs Herriton in *Where Angels Fear to Tread* she is
one of Forster's matriarchal figures, cold, heartless, life-denying
and fond of imposing her will on others. (One feels that it is
only a matter of time before Agnes joins the group.) Forster's
diagnosis of her nature is wittily devastating:

> She imagined herself to be a cold-eyed Scandinavian heroine
> [i.e. like one of Ibsen's forceful women characters such as
> Hedda Gabler]. Really she was an old English lady, who did
> not mind giving other people a chill provided it was not
> infectious.

Stephen, who lives with her, is a young man of obscure origins
who has been taken up by Mr Failing and is tolerated by Mrs
Failing: an unpolished youth with a love of outdoor life, he is
capable of being mistaken for a peasant, and Rickie later thinks
of him as 'a kind of cynical ploughboy' (Ch. 23). One critic has
called him 'a sort of English Gino'.

Into this strange household Rickie and Agnes arrive on a
visit soon after their engagement. Just before they reach their
destination, the train in which they are travelling runs over and
kills a child playing on a level-crossing; a somewhat obscure
connection is hinted at between the child's death and the fact

that, as the accident takes place, Rickie and Agnes are embracing. At the very least, though, the implied connection between their love and the child's death seems ominous; and the incident, slight though it seems at the time, forms part of an important pattern of events, since first their own child is to die and later Rickie is to be killed at the same spot. Here Forster shows considerable power in endowing an incident that seems marginal to the main action with resonance and in using it as part of a developing pattern within the novel. It becomes clear that the accident would not have occurred if there had been a bridge over the line, and Stephen tells Mrs Failing passionately that she ought to have paid for the construction of a bridge. This tiny episode puts to the test the characters of four people, and their varying reactions tell us a good deal about their essential natures: Rickie is genuinely troubled but tries to argue that it must have been another train that killed the child, as if that would relieve him of the moral responsibility that he seems to feel; Agnes, untroubled by the tragedy, briskly tries to change the subject, 'for she saw that it made Rickie unhappy'; Mrs Failing is callously indifferent and unrepentant; Stephen cares deeply about the rights and wrongs of the matter and about personal responsibility – for him it is 'your train' that caused the death. We may note that Rickie's and Stephen's reactions, though not identical, have something in common (and this may hint at the relationship between them, to be revealed later); also that masculine concern is contrasted with female indifference.

Physically and temperamentally, Rickie and Stephen could hardly be more different; the latter's 'brutality' reminds Rickie of Gerald, but Stephen has none of the dead man's snobbishness – a child of nature or a noble savage, he seems a worthy product of Mr Failing's idealistic egalitarian doctrines. The contrast between Rickie and Stephen is dramatised when they ride together to Salisbury: Rickie, inept in managing his horse and shocked by Stephen's vulgarity, abandons the expedition and returns to the womenfolk, while Stephen exchanges badinage (at Mrs Failing's expense) with a drunken soldier and becomes involved in a fight. Again Forster seems to want the reader to take on trust an idea that is not adequately dramatised: that Stephen's life is lived so unselfconsciously and instinctively, and is so closely bound up with the Wiltshire landscape, that he is almost a personification of natural forces, and that whereas

Rickie writes clever little stories about the power of nature asserting itself, Stephen genuinely embodies that power.

The climax of the visit to Cadover comes at the end of Chapter 13, when Mrs Failing, apparently in a moment of impulsive malice or troublemaking, tells Rickie that Stephen is his half-brother. Again we have a situation in which character is put to the test. When Rickie tells Agnes, her instinct is to hush the matter up: Mrs Failing, already regretting her rash act, has sent Stephen away for a time, and Agnes is prepared to conspire with her (women once more in alliance against men and against the truth) to keep Stephen in ignorance of the relationship. Rickie, however, reacts in a way that invokes the values of Cambridge rather than those of Sawston, when he insists to Agnes:

> 'But she can't behave to people like that. She must tell him.'
> 'Why?'
> 'Because he must be told such a real thing.'

That final phrase recalls, of course, the opening scene of the novel, and Ansell would not be surprised to learn that Agnes does not know what Rickie is talking about. Then comes a crucial moment of moral choice: it appears that Stephen has after all not yet left Cadover, for he calls up from the drive to say goodbye to Rickie. Rickie has only to speak to him to make him aware of 'such a real thing' and moves forward, presumably to do so, but Agnes intervenes, 'stopping his advance quite frankly, with outspread arms', and Rickie is struck by her beauty. In the struggle between his sexual passion and his passion for the truth, sex wins. It is one of the turning-points of Rickie's life, this moment of inaction. He tears up a letter to Ansell in which he has confided the momentous discovery. In the struggle for possession of Rickie (and there is something almost demonic about Agnes 'with outspread arms') Sawston has won a victory over Cambridge. In Forster's portentous phrase, 'the woman had conquered'.

Soon afterwards, Rickie has 'a curious breakdown' (Ch. 15), and then tries, without success, to get his stories published. A well-meaning editor tells him to 'see life' in order to become a better writer (something that Forster himself may have felt the need of doing), but Rickie has by now turned his back on life and reality, and 'the heart of all things was hidden' from him. This concludes the first section of the novel which, although titled 'Cambridge', has also introduced the other two settings that, in their different ways, serve as contrasts to Cambridge. If the medieval university city represents the life of intellect and culture, the disinterested quest for truth and the holiness of personal relationships, especially male friendships, Sawston and Wiltshire offer alternative choices of ways to live: the one belongs to the aggressive modern spirit of competition and worldly success (it is suggestive that the original purpose of the ancient school, to educate poor boys, has been lost sight of in the process of its transformation into a public school for the Victorian *nouveaux riches* and rising professional classes), while the other stands for closeness to the natural world, for history and prehistory (we are often reminded of Wiltshire's Iron Age sites and Roman roads), and for a mode of life in which instinct and direct physical experience are ranked above rationality and intellectualism (Forster here anticipating the ideas of D. H. Lawrence).

By the mid-point of the novel, then, Rickie has thrown in his lot with Sawston: by marrying Agnes, taking a job at the school, and supporting Herbert in his petty power-struggles with other masters, he commits himself to Sawston values – or, to put it the other way round, turns his back on those of Cambridge. At this point it can be seen quite clearly how unswervingly and wholeheartedly Forster is a *moralist*: a long tradition of English novels from *Tom Jones* to *Jude the Obscure* traces the fluctuations in the fortunes of their heroes, and these fortunes are seen, to a significant extent, in social and economic terms. By choosing to write about those who already belong to the middle class, Forster excludes class-mobility (though not class-consciousness) as a major preoccupation of his fiction: whereas, for instance, Paul Morel in Lawrence's *Sons and Lovers* is motivated to a significant extent by his aspirations to the middle-class intelligentsia and the 'life of ideas', Rickie Elliot takes his membership of this class for granted, and *his* struggles are depicted as ethical rather than social.

In Sawston, Rickie comes under the influence of Herbert Pembroke, whose portrait is sharply ironic in the manner of Jane Austen. Herbert's beginning-of-term exhortations to the boys are hollow and cliché-ridden: his morality is a matter of unthinking formulae and catch-phrases, his real nature self-seeking and self-deceiving. In Chapter 16 he decides that it might be useful to his career as a housemaster if he were to get married, and in this spirit of calculation he finds an eligible widow apparently available and persuades himself that what he can offer her is 'a nobler, riper emotion' than youthful passion. The truth is that he feels nothing at all, and the narrator comments: 'It never took him long to get muddled, or to reverse cause and effect.' (For a comment on Forster's addiction to the word 'muddle', see p. 48 above.)

Agnes is, of course, on the same side as her brother and determinedly pulls Rickie back when he shows signs of reverting to his former ideals and values. In Chapter 19 she firmly nips in the bud his developing friendship with Mr Jackson, another master, whose tastes are similar to Rickie's. She also points out that Jackson is 'in the reactionary camp' and that 'we must hang together'; Rickie is thus forced into taking sides in the petty politics of the school rather than acting as his sense of what is right prompts him. As in the earlier scene when Rickie failed to tell Stephen the truth, Forster makes it clear that the potency of Agnes' sexual attraction is partly to blame for Rickie's lapse: like Samson, he is betrayed to the philistines by a woman.

Some perspective on Rickie's situation at this low point in his moral existence is given by the scene in Chapter 20 in which his Cambridge friends, Ansell and Widdrington, meet in the Reading Room of the British Museum. Widdrington has recently visited Sawston and reports that Rickie is totally absorbed in the affairs of the school; as for Agnes, she is like an electric light in her inhuman efficiency. Ansell, who has professed from the start to disbelieve in Agnes's existence, now doubts whether Rickie is any longer a real person. But it must be said that Rickie is not a mere pawn in the competent hands of his wife and his brother-in-law: if he were wholly passive he would lack the interest and complexity that we rightly demand of a protagonist, and there is in his assent to Sawston values an element of self-deception. By Chapter 21, however, the mists (to use Forster's metaphor) begin to clear: he realises that his heart is not in the profession of teaching and that he and Agnes have no deep love for each other – in short, he is beginning to perceive the reality of things. At the same time he faces a crisis in his life: he has longed for a son, but when the baby is born it is a girl and is seriously deformed. The child soon dies (adding to the mounting toll of deaths in the novel), but Rickie vows that he must never again risk fathering another child, and although Forster does not make the point explicitly, we may suppose that his fear of transmitting the hereditary defect will bring to an end his sexual life with Agnes.

Mrs Failing and Stephen, who have disappeared from the novel for a time, are reintroduced by a rather clumsy device (thanks to a combination of misunderstandings and coincidence, Stephen corresponds with a boy at the school), and Agnes's bourgeois obsession with wealth, property and inheritance – a theme to reappear in *Howards End* – leads her to suggest that Rickie should make up the quarrel with his aunt. Rickie, who has by now acquired a disillusioned skill in reading Agnes's character, penetrates her hypocrisy and accurately detects her motive: she wants Rickie to figure in the old lady's will. Rickie is emboldened to revive the question of telling Stephen about their relationship, and this leads to their first quarrel. The marriage is now deteriorating rapidly, for although they make up and Rickie retracts his threat to write to his half-brother, 'he knew that they had destroyed the habit of reverence, and would quarrel again'.

Chapter 23 ends with a paragraph in Forster's most sternly moralistic manner:

Henceforward he deteriorates. Let those who censure him suggest what he should do. He has lost the work that he loved, his friends, and his child. He remained conscientious and decent, but the spiritual part of him proceeded towards ruin.

This is confusing and seems to represent a zigzagging of Forster's purpose. How can we reconcile it with the reference a little earlier to Rickie's emergence from the 'mists', with his new-found readiness to stand up to Agnes's ladylike bullying, and with the self-scrutiny and self-knowledge that have come to him during a night of spiritual agony? It would seem more reasonable to suppose that Rickie's awareness of the failure of his marriage – a facing of the truth at last – is the beginning of his salvation. Here and sometimes elsewhere, Forster's argument is hard to follow: indeed, it is not so much an argument as a series of assertions and one has the sense of something unexplained, of an attempt to convey the mystery and complexity of life that succeeds only in teasing, baffling and perhaps exasperating the reader.

Matters between the couple come to a head in a supper-table scene in Chapter 25; the kind of exposure of domestic discord that, again, Forster must have learned at least partly from Jane Austen. During a recent visit by Mrs Failing, Agnes has revealed to her what she had been told in confidence by Rickie – that Stephen had spoken disrespectfully of his patroness to a drunken soldier during his visit to Salisbury – and Mrs Failing's response has been to tell Stephen that he must emigrate to Canada. Rickie now accuses his wife of betraying his confidence in the interests of legacy-hunting, and tells her that she has 'ruined Stephen'.

Coincidence is again resorted to in Chapter 26, where Ansell and Stephen meet in Sawston and indulge in a not very serious fight: one of those curious Forsterian encounters that seem to act as a kind of metaphor for intimacy and communion (Lawrence, as we saw, uses the same device in *Women in Love*). Stephen tells Ansell that he has been turned out of Cadover; Mrs Failing has given him a hundred pounds, but he quixotically refuses to touch it. She has also given him a packet of letters, from which he has learned that Rickie is his half-brother and, not knowing that this is no secret to Rickie, has come to tell him the news. But he is intercepted by Agnes, who has armed herself with a blank cheque already signed by Rickie: she assumes (and the assumption is of course very revealing) that Stephen has come as a blackmailer, and is ready to buy him off. Stephen's simple but strong code of morality scorns such an idea and he leaves. Ansell is now invited to stay for lunch and joins Rickie in the school dining-hall, where a curious scene takes place – a scene that some have regarded as so improbable that it has been described as 'operatic' (Leavis dismisses it, less indulgently, as 'crudely unreal').

There are certainly elements in it that can fairly be called melodramatic: for instance, the stagy flavour of some of the dialogue, such as Herbert's 'Out of my sight, sir! . . . Sir, I give you two minutes, then you will be expelled by force'. One

cannot help thinking that a real-life Herbert (and the
effectiveness of this character arises from the fact that he is no
Dickensian grotesque but an accurate and convincing portrayal
of a familiar English type) would have tried to hush the affair
up rather than joining in a debate, even one limited to two
minutes, before the assembled boys. The climax of the scene
brings the revelation from Ansell that Stephen is the son of
Rickie's mother, whose memory Rickie has idealised, not (as
Rickie had supposed) of his father. This is an extra turn of the
screw, since Rickie's earlier discovery that he had a half-brother
who was the product of his father's adultery is now shown to be
only partially true: Rickie, who has wanted Stephen to know
'such a real thing', is himself forced to confront a reality more
painful than he had imagined possible. And this has come
about as a result of the Cambridge conviction, personified by
Ansell, that one should not only see things as they are but
should tell the truth with complete candour.

Part 3 opens with a flashback to a period many years before
the main action of the novel begins, and its purpose is to
provide an explanation of what has just been revealed and to
show the influence of the past on the present. Rickie's mother,
married to a heartless and unfaithful man, was loved by and at
last had an affair with 'a young farmer of some education'
called Robert, who was fairly promptly drowned in a bathing
accident. (The reader may well feel by this point that being a
character in *The Longest Journey* is a high-risk occupation.) Rickie,
at first shattered by the truth, now moves towards 'a new life'
(Ch. 31), as if purged and purified by his knowledge and
suffering. In Chapter 33, he and Stephen return to Cadover
together: they indulge in horseplay in a railway carriage
(perhaps we are expected to recall Rickie's last railway journey,
with Agnes), and sail paper boats on a stream, as if trying to
make up for the missed opportunities of brotherly companionship
in their boyhood. But the idyll is short-lived: Stephen breaks
his promise to Rickie that he will not drink and, finding him
drunk, Rickie is strangely affected by his failure to keep his
word. His reaction, indeed, seems excessive: he describes
Stephen as 'suddenly ruined', and declares that he himself has
made a terrible mistake in 'trusting the earth' and 'pretend[ing]
again that people were real'. Incurably idealistic, Rickie has
tried to make a hero or a myth out of his half-brother, whereas

Stephen is not an incarnation of the spirit of the landscape, only a likeable but all too fallible human being.

In despair, Rickie realises that, after this brief interlude of escape into what he has believed to be an ideal world of male comradeship, nothing remains for him but to return to his wife: 'he knew that the conventions would claim him soon' (Ch. 34). This echoes, but at the same time contradicts, an insight he has been afforded a few pages earlier: 'He . . . knew that conventions are not majestic, and that they will not claim us in the end.' To have sent Rickie back to Agnes would have given the novel a bleak, uncompromising, but not implausible ending. What Forster actually does, however, is to resort yet again to sudden calamity: finding Stephen lying drunk on the railway line as a train approaches, Rickie rescues him, only to be killed by the train himself.

What are we to make of this conclusion? Rickie, it is made clear, has tried to save his own life, but out of a sense of duty rather than impulse, for he has nothing to live for. That he has saved Stephen, however, sets a seal on their relationship and endows Rickie with a heroism that he has hardly achieved in life. The conclusion has been foreshadowed as early as Chapter 10, where Stephen has urged the need for a bridge over the dangerous level-crossing. Rickie has not succeeded in building a bridge between Stephen's life and his own, but his death has not been useless. For after a scene (Ch. 35) in which Herbert is shown trying to get more than his fair share of the royalties on Rickie's posthumously-published book – here is one character at least who may suffer but will never change – the novel ends with a reference to Stephen's child. (Forster will later use a very similar ending in *Howards End*.) The child affirms the continuity of family and race, and seems to promise a future in which humanity may learn wisdom, so that the ending may be regarded as expressing a qualified optimism. Rickie was determined not to become a father again, but his blood-relationship to Stephen's child, and hence in some sense his survival, are commemorated in the little girl's name, which is that of their mother (and 'mother' is the last word of the novel). A point of significance in this final scene is that Stephen is taking the child to sleep out 'on the hillside' – away, that is, from the indoor world of women and philosophers (Ansell seems to be staying, or perhaps living, with them), into a close intimacy with the earth and into the darkness in which, it may be, Rickie is to be found.

This necessarily lengthy account of what happens in *The Longest Journey* suggests one of its most obvious features, and one of its weaknesses. Forster is exploring a moral theme – the conflict of ideals and worldliness, of truth and convention, of the urge for personal freedom and spontaneous feeling and the pressure of conformity and class codes – yet he chooses to conduct his exploration through a huddle of episodes against which the complaint must be that they not only resort to improbability and melodrama but that they are often quite perfunctorily presented. It is almost as if he were bored with plot-making and the construction of narrative. An example of this occurs at the end of Chapter 30, when Rickie saves Stephen's life: the incident is over in a dozen words or so, it could easily be missed by a momentarily inattentive reader, and one wonders why Forster bothered to include it. Throughout the novel, Forster draws on the stock-in-trade of the old-fashioned heavily-plotted fictional tradition, including adultery, skeletons in family cupboards, sudden death, coincidence and the like, whereas the novel he really wants to write seems to be of quite a different kind, shorter and less sensational, with more use of poetic symbol and less of incident and the twists and turns of a complex plot. It is as if, wishing to write fiction in the manner of Virginia Woolf, he finds himself lapsing into the manner of a minor Victorian novelist.

Another way in which *The Longest Journey* may seem unsatisfactory to present-day readers is its frequent indulgence, especially at moments of heightened significance, in romantic rhetoric, replete with high-flown abstractions and poetic imagery. A fair sample is the very short chapter (28) that ends the second part: the reader who expects a clear-eyed analysis of Rickie's condition at this crucial moment in his experience is fobbed off with a highly 'literary' essay on 'the soul'. Leavis found Forster's 'poetic communication about life . . . almost unbelievably crude and weak'; there is also something strangely dated about the writing in such passages, which seem to have strayed from some once-popular but now unreadable turn-of-the-century volume of *belles lettres*. In such passages Forster was no doubt influenced by George Meredith (1828–1909), a poet and novelist whose work once enjoyed enormous popularity and of whom Walter Allen has said that his novels were 'merely one form his poetry took'. In *Aspects of the Novel* (1927), Forster compares Meredith unfavourably to Hardy, who is also an influence on the Wiltshire scenes of *The Longest Journey*; he also describes Meredith's 'visions of nature' as 'fluffy and lush', and detects in his work 'the home counties posing as the universe', but the gibe can be turned back on his own novel. For compared with Hardy's, Forster's feeling for nature seems bookish and cerebral; as Colmer points out, late-Victorian and Edwardian writers such as Richard Jefferies (a Wiltshire farmer's son) and W. H. Hudson who 'celebrated the spirit of the earth' were an important influence.

Peter Widdowson has said of *Howards End*, Forster's fourth novel:

> A movement between 'realistic' specificity and generalising rhetoric (especially at points when 'realism' is inapposite or inadequate) is characteristic of the novel as a whole, and bears witness to its uncertainty of mode.[45]

This uncertainty of mode is to be found also in *The Longest Journey*, as it is not, on the whole, in the less ambitious but more assured 'Italian' novels.

Despite these weaknesses, though, there is much of the essential Forster in this novel. The 'symbolic moment, which, if a man accepts, he has accepted life' (Ch. 31) is the opportunity given to each to embrace life in its fullest reality, which involves a courageous rejection of mere conformity and all insincerity. Probably Forster's concern with this theme was given urgency by his awareness of the compromises of his personal guilt. The title of the novel is, as already noted, taken from Shelley's poem *Epipsychidion*, and the relevant passage, quoted in Chapter 13, pleads for a view of human relationships unrestricted by the institution of marriage and in which friendship is an essential part of life. As Stephen puts it in Chapter 33, 'all one's thoughts can't belong to any single person'. These are themes that recur in Forster's later work: to the end of his career as a novelist, he continues to re-explore the nature of salvation and the need for friendship, and to divide mankind into the lost and the saved.

4

Howards End

For Lionel Trilling, *Howards End* (1910) is 'undoubtedly Forster's masterpiece'; for F. R. Leavis, it 'exhibits crudity of a kind to shock and distress the reader as Mr Forster hasn't shocked or distressed him before'.[46] When two of the twentieth century's most distinguished critics take up such sharply contrasting positions, we can expect to encounter critical problems in our consideration of this work. What seems undeniable, however, is that of the four novels Forster had published to date, *Howards End* is the most ambitious.

At the same time, it is far from representing a development in a totally new direction, and there is an obvious continuity with his earlier work. As Furbank has said, 'Forster had relatively few fictional patterns and was content to use those he knew again and again'.[47] Colmer notes that *Howards End* 'takes up and expands the theme touched on at the end of *The Longest Journey*: who shall inherit England?',[48] and as we examine the later novel we find certain features already familiar from our discussion of its predecessors. Just as the worlds of Cambridge and Sawston (and in the 'Italian' novels England and Italy) had been contrasted and then brought together by marriage, Forster now first contrasts the world of the Schlegels and the Wilcoxes and then unites them through Margaret's marriage to Henry Wilcox. The spirit of place is again strong, Howards End embodying a way of life and a system of values as, for instance, Cambridge and Wiltshire had done earlier. And the novel opens with the well-tried device of the 'rescue party' and returns to the same device near its end.

Where it goes beyond its predecessors is partly in its wider social range – Leonard and Jackie Bast have no real counterparts in the earlier work – and partly in its more contemporary feel. In reading *Howards End* we are more conscious of the date of

composition and the presumed date of the action than in
reading its predecessors. This is partly because of references to
such questions of the day as women's suffrage and such new
phenomena as the motor-car, but the topicality is more pervasive
than these specific instances suggest. Some commentators have
suggested that it may be seen as a fictional counterpart to, for
instance, C. F. G. Masterman's widely-read *The Condition of
England* (1909). Although there are a number of interesting
parallels between the two books, what is important is not the
question of 'influence' or indebtedness but the fact that two
writers should respond in such similar ways to the social context
of their age, despite the difference of backgrounds and genres
(Masterman was a Liberal MP and his book is a work of
political and sociological analysis). As Peter Widdowson has
said, 'The similarity of their position is at times uncanny'.[49]

The first reference to the novel that was to become *Howards
End* occurs in an entry in Forster's diary dated 26 June 1908,
where he outlines an 'idea for another novel' (*A Room with a
View* had presumably been completed, but had not yet been
published, at this time):

> In a prelude Helen goes to stop with the Wilcoxes, gets
> engaged to the son & breaks it off immediately, for her
> instinct sees the spiritual cleavage between the families. Mrs
> Wilcox dies, and some 2 years later Margaret gets engaged to
> the widower, a man impeccable publicly. They are accosted
> by a prostitute. M., because she understands & is great,
> marries him. The wrong thing to do. He, because he is little,
> cannot bear to be understood, & goes to the bad. He is frank,
> kind, & attractive. But he dreads ideas.[50]

Obviously, this is far from being a synopsis of the novel that
was eventually written: for example, it contains nothing about
Helen's baby and the piece of plot-mechanism involving an
encounter with a prostitute is transformed into the major
element of the novel that concerns the Basts. But it is striking
that, though Forster will later expand and develop the *story*, the
moral basis of the novel is already established, if only in its
starkest and most abstract outlines: the 'spiritual cleavage
between the families', Margaret's 'greatness', Henry's dread of

'ideas' and the attempt to reconcile opposites through marriage give the story its moral framework.

About six months earlier, another diary entry gives a clue to what I have already referred to as the strong contemporary flavour of the novel, and an insight into Forster's attitudes to a rapidly changing world – attitudes that were to be presented dramatically in his novel. On 13 January 1908, a Frenchman named Henri Farman had flown a heavier-than-air machine for three-quarters of a mile in ninety seconds; and this news item prompted Forster to write:

> It really *is* a new civilisation. I have been born at the end of the age of peace and can't expect to feel anything but despair. . . . God what a prospect! The little houses that I am used to will be swept away, the fields will stink of petrol, and the airships will shatter the stars.[51]

As Oliver Stallybrass has pointed out, during this year Forster wrote his short story 'The Machine Stops', which represents a counterblast to the cheerful futuristic vision of H. G. Wells. *Howards End* embodies both a satirical attack on the 'new civilisation' represented by the motorcar (the phrase 'stink of petrol' in the above entry is echoed in 'the throbbing, stinking car' at the end of Chapter 3, significantly associated with the Wilcoxes) and an evocation of the very different way of life, tranquil and predominantly rural ('The little houses . . . the fields . . .'), of his childhood.

It is only by an effort of the historical imagination that we can recapture something of his feelings; for, from the point of view of the late twentieth century, the Edwardian age has itself become the object of romantic nostalgia, and has been presented in these terms not only in numerous television costume dramas and soap operas but in, for example, Philip Larkin's poem 'MCMXIV', which evokes the world that ended with the outbreak of the Great War through the use of details strikingly reminiscent of Forster's novel:

> And the countryside not caring:
> The place-names all hazed over
> With flowering grasses, and fields

> Shadowing Domesday lines
> Under wheat's restless silence;
> The differently-dressed servants
> With tiny rooms in huge houses,
> The dust behind limousines; . . .

While we contemplate the age down the long perspective of twentieth-century history, however, for Forster in 1908–10 it was the here and now, and formed a sad contrast with the world he saw vanishing. No doubt his feelings were partly accounted for by the fact that the vanishing world was not just a portion of history but the period of his own spoiled and happy childhood: he was thirty in 1909, an age at which many people become acutely conscious of the passing of time. Although he lived well into the atomic age, and responded eloquently to the profound changes in civilisation, Forster remained in many respects a Victorian or Edwardian: not only in his appearance, his style of dress and his accent but in such matters as his attitude to children and servants, he represented in his later years a survival from a much earlier perid.

Victoria's death in the first month of the new century had been seen by many as the end of an epoch; and long before the death of her son Edward VII in 1910 there were signs of social change at home and, even more ominously, the threat of German militarism. Within a very few years, the 'airships' referred to in the diary entry quoted above would be transformed from amusing toys into instruments of war widely known as Zeppelins. In *Howards End* this spirit of change is represented by the internal combustion engine, bringing noise and the smell of petrol fumes to England's quiet lanes. (To intrude a personal note, my father, born in 1898, as a small boy in a Northamptonshire village saw his first motor-car one day while out playing in the quiet road, and to the end of his life recalled it as a noisy and slowly advancing cloud of dust – exactly the terms in which Forster presents the phenomenon.) Nor is it merely a contemporary detail, for it functions as a recurring symbol of the Wilcox world and is thus integrated with the main theme of the novel.

If the new England is symbolised by a moving vehicle, the traditional England is represented by a number of places based on personal associations. The most important of these is the house that gives its name to the book. Howards End is modelled on Rooksnest, where Forster spent most of his boyhood (see p. 2 above); the house still stands but the wych-elm, clearly visible in an early photograph, and in the novel both a realistic detail and a symbol of continuity, is no more. Another house of importance is the London home of the Schlegels, located in 'Wickham Place' but apparently based on Goldsworthy Lowes Dickinson's house in All Souls Place. (There is, again, an obvious symbolism in the lease of the Schlegel home running out.) A third location, Oniton, is based on Clun in Shropshire, which Forster had visited in the spring of 1907. Clun is commemorated in A. E. Housman's *A Shropshire Lad* (1896), a collection of poems that itself expresses regret for a vanished and idealised world.

Work on the new novel seems to have begun soon after the diary entry of 26 June 1908 and continued during the next two years, so that by the end of July 1910 it was 'nearly done'. Some four months earlier Forster had sent a draft of about two-thirds of the novel to his publisher, and the response had been favourable. One criticism that had been made, however, concerned the handling of Helen's relationship with Leonard Bast. Forster himself had not been satisfied with this episode, and for different reasons, moral rather than artistic, his mother had been 'deeply shocked'. As we shall see later, reviewers also found fault with it, and for many readers it remains a blemish – moreover, as I shall suggest, a blemish of a rather characteristic kind.

As a whole, however, the book was very well received when it appeared: Forster, who had now published four novels in six years and was only thirty-one, found himself looked to as one of the most important novelists of his generation – a mantle, it must be said, that he was distinctly uneasy at wearing. (For further comments on the reception of *Howards End*, see p. 9 above.) Towards the end of his life, Forster expressed rather mixed feelings regarding it:

Howards End my best novel and approaching a good novel. Very elaborate and all pervading plot that is seldom tiresome or forced, range of characters, social sense, wit, wisdom, colour. Have only just discovered why I don't care for it: not a single character in it for whom I care. . . . I feel pride in the achievement, but I cannot love it.[52]

His account of the book's virtues seems generally acceptable, though his unquestioning approval of an 'elaborate and all pervading plot' may not be shared by every reader: for some this novel, like *The Longest Journey*, might have benefited from being a little less heavily plotted, and some of the best scenes are those in which the twists and turns of the story are least prominent.

Plot, with Forster, often seems extrinsic and almost fortuitous, as if applied from the outside and at the last moment (we shall find evidence of this when we consider the ending of the novel) rather than being shaped as an expression or embodiment of the novel's themes. What are more interesting are the structural principles that underlie the deployment of character, incident and setting; and here we find ourselves on familiar ground, for Forster turns again to symmetries and antitheses similar to those used in his earlier novels.

As R. N. Parkinson has said, in writing this novel Forster 'seems to have felt in terms of antitheses'.[53] The central antithesis this time is not between two places but between two families, the Schlegels and the Wilcoxes. The former are cultured, humane, liberal and enlightened in their views; fortified by an unearned income, they pursue a life devoted to intellectual and aesthetic interests – in all these respects resembling Forster himself, though unlike him they are half-German. Their surname is that of a famous German philosopher and literary critic, and reminds us that in the nineteenth century Germany was culturally and intellectually in the forefront of European civilisation. Their father, we learn in Chapter 4, was 'the countryman of Hegel and Kant' and 'the idealist, inclined to be dreamy', a type that recalls Mr Emerson and Mr Failing in earlier novels. The Wilcoxes belong to a slightly different section of the middle class and are in human terms as different as it is possible to be from the Schlegels. Affluent, energetic, successful, and when necessary ruthless, theirs is the world of large-scale business enterprises. A recurring phrase that becomes attached to them is 'telegrams and anger':

they habitually resort to decisive action and dogmatic, intolerant convictions.

Although it may appear initially as if Schlegel virtues are to be contrasted with Wilcox shortcomings, the truth turns out to be somewhat more complex than this: troubled by a sense of guilt at their privileged lives, Margaret Schlegel comes to wonder whether the leisure enjoyed by her and her sister and brother does not perhaps make for a kind of softness or ineffectuality, and she correspondingly comes to feel an admiration, emotional rather than rational, for the Wilcox energy and ability to get things done.

This central antithesis, then, does not remain a stable presence throughout the book but is qualified and modified: the reader who is ready to succumb to the easy temptation of choosing between sharply-defined opposites finds himself forced to hesitate and to say, 'Yes, but. . .'. There is nevertheless a strong sense of two sets of principles and values, two views of how life should be lived in the conditions of modern civilisation; but the moral action of the novel takes place in the space between the two rather than urging the claims of one at the expense of the other. Ultimately, though, Forster finds himself in the position of having to cast a vote and it will not surprise us that he plumps for the defeat of the Wilcoxes. In the process, however, Margaret Schlegel's own position has shifted significantly. Peter Widdowson finds in *Howards End* a 'rich ambiguity' and a 'fundamental *irresolution*', and it may be that we should see the novel as not so much presenting a case as conducting a debate. In this respect it seems to go beyond the earlier novels, where the antitheses are more pronounced and emphatic, and the author's confidence that he is in possession of a truth admitting no qualification is liable to grate a little, or more than a little, on his readers. That nothing good can come out of Sawston, or that all Italians have a profound understanding of how to live, are claims apt to strike us as grossly exaggerated and over-simplified and the subjects of such generalisations often have an air of unreality. As Trilling has said, in reading the early novels 'we can sometimes see that their assumptions have been right but rather too easy'; *Howards End*, on the other hand, 'develops to the full the themes and attitudes of the early books and throws back upon them a new

enhancing light. It justifies these attitudes by connecting them
with a more mature sense of responsibility.'[54]

Forster explores ways in which the gap between the two
terms of the central antithesis can be bridged. The metaphor of
a bridge is an important one in his work (the symbolic missing
bridge over the railway line in *The Longest Journey* has already
been noted), and it is implicit in the brief but pregnant epigraph
of *Howards End*: 'Only connect . . .', which comes to acquire a
rich and multiple significance as the novel proceeds. There is
nothing new about 'connecting' as a theme or structural
principle in fiction and the Victorian novel, with its plots and
subplots and its panoramic social range, had lent itself especially
well to displaying the hidden but vital connections in human
life. In a key passage of *Bleak House* (1853), for instance,
Dickens's narrator demands rhetorically, 'What connexion can
there have been between many people in the innumerable
histories of this world, who, from opposite sides of great gulfs,
have, nevertheless, been very curiously brought together!', and
then goes on to show the physical and moral reality of the
interrelationships of those at opposite ends of London society;
and in a similarly important passage in *Middlemarch* (1872),
George Eliot refers to 'the stealthy convergence of human lots'
that seem superficially unconnected. Forster does not confront
the 'great gulfs' of society, but he is equally concerned with the
theme of 'connection'. Moreover he goes beyond these precedents
in seeing connection as not only proceeding from the workings
of fate, providence or unconscious impulses, but as something
to be worked for and felt as a binding duty – a moral imperative
reflected in the grammatical imperative of his 'Only connect. . .'.

The opening chapters present the two families, and even
before their respective qualities have been delineated there has
been a brief abortive attempt to unite them – a point that will
not be reached again until halfway through the novel. *Howards
End* opens more dramatically than any of Forster's other novels,
as Helen first announces (at the end of Chapter 1) that she is in
love with Paul Wilcox, then (at the end of Chapter 2) sends a
telegram – the Wilcox drive is infectious – to say 'All over'. But by
this time Aunt Juley (Mrs Munt) has set off, a one-woman rescue
party, and a comedy of errors ensues. Forster's art in these
opening pages has an admirable economy and unobtrusiveness:
by the end of three short chapters the reader has been introduced

to nearly all the main characters and has been made aware of qualities, such as Helen's impulsiveness and Charles's assertiveness, that will turn out to have far-reaching effects.

Nor is this all, for Forster has introduced, on a level different from those of character and situation, motifs that will recur and give the book a symbolic unity. On the second page Helen describes Mrs Wilcox 'with her hands full of the hay that was cut yesterday'; the detail is referred to a second time in the same passage; even before this, we have learned that both Charles Wilcox and Tibby Schlegel suffer from hayfever, and the reference to this affliction is also very quickly repeated, as if these allusions were a musical theme appearing and reappearing in slightly different but still recognisable forms. Repetition serves to bring to our attention the significance of the apparently random detail and the references to hay will recur from time to time until the final appearance of this motif in the last sentence of the novel. Again, in Chapter 3 we are given an account of Charles's drive from the railway station to the Wilcox home and this is both a brilliant, detailed and historically fascinating picture of the early days of motoring and a symbol of the Wilcox power and indifference to others: they are the new men who, like the new machines, are irreversibly transforming the face of England.

These two symbols are worth reflecting on, for in their own way they constitute another example of the use of antithesis as a structural device in this novel. The hay stands for rural England, the natural world with its seasonal rhythms and rich sensuous appeal, and a treasured sense of tradition and the past. To put it in this abstract fashion is, however, to deprive the symbol of its force, for the hay that Mrs Wilcox carries and sniffs is evoked as a physical presence, its fragrance providing a sensory link with other haymakings in the past of the individual and the race. That it cannot be tolerated by the other Wilcoxes both marks off the mother from her husband and sons and implies that the men of the family – those whose successful efforts in the world of business have brought material rewards – have cut themselves off from the natural world and the past. We learn in Chapter 33 that 'There's not one Wilcox that can stand up against a field in June'. Mrs Wilcox is of course a Wilcox only by marriage: her maiden name was Howard, connecting her with the house she has inherited. (A point of

interest in the manuscript of the novel is that hay was not at
first associated with Mrs Wilcox – the positive aspect of the
symbol – though the negative aspect, the hayfever, is there at
an early stage.)

Allergic to hay, and profoundly out of sympathy with nature
and tradition, the Wilcox males are filled with enthusiasm by
the internal combustion engine. Forster conveys very vividly
the impact of these strange and noisy vehicles on Edwardian
England, rather as Dickens a couple of generations earlier had
registered the impact of the railways in *Dombey and Son*. The
Oxford English Dictionary records the words *motor-car* and
automobile as appearing in 1895 and the Automobile Club was
founded in 1897, so that motoring was still very much a novelty
in Forster's youth and even when *Howards End* was written. As
Chapter 3 shows clearly, even a short journey by car was an
elaborate business calling for 'gloves and spectacles', 'rugs and
shawls', raising a 'cloud of dust', and attracting attention from
bystanders. Cars at this time were expensive, and that the
Wilcoxes possess one indicates their affluence as well as their
eagerness to ally themselves with mechanical 'progress'. What
Forster is recording in this episode and in subsequent references
to the car is nothing less than a dramatic change in the quality
and rhythms of life. Twenty-eight chapters later he will refer to
the 'nomadic civilisation' that he saw emerging, and in the final
chapter of the novel to the modern 'craze for motion'. The
increased mobility and access to even the remoter corners of the
English countryside made possible by the motor-car was a
major instrument of this upheaval.

Nor was it just a matter of physical motion: the very nature
and quality of human perception were undergoing modification.
Most striking of all in Forster's depiction of the advent of the
motor-car age is the sense of speed, of the world rushing past
the driver or passenger more rapidly than the senses or the
mind can react to it or absorb its meaning. (At the time, it is
true, cars travelled much more slowly than trains; nevertheless
the sense of speed in an open car, and the proximity to streets,
houses and pedestrians, made motoring an entirely new kind of
experience.) Speed, noise, what we should call pollution, and
danger are in the process of transforming a rural world that, as
late-Victorian and Edwardian photographs often suggest, had

not radically changed in centuries. Forster evokes this spirit of change by a masterly use of detail:

> Charles contemplated the cloud of dust that they had raised in their passage through the village. It was settling again, but not all into the road from which he had taken it. Some of it had percolated through the open windows, some had whitened the roses and gooseberries of the wayside gardens, while a certain proportion had entered the lungs of the villagers. 'I wonder when they'll learn wisdom and tar the roads,' was his comment. (Ch. 3)

The reference to the 'roses' is echoed at the end of the same chapter when Mrs Wilcox bends down 'to smell a rose'.

Another passage much later in the novel may be quoted here as reinforcing Forster's vision of the motor-car as not just another mechanical invention but a means of altering – considerably for the worse – the quality of human perceptions and responses:

> The chauffeur could not travel as quickly as he had hoped, for the Great North Road was full of Easter traffic. But he went quite quick enough for Margaret, a poor-spirited creature, who had chickens and children on the brain.
>
> 'They're all right,' said Mr Wilcox. 'They'll learn – like swallows and the telegraph-wires.'
>
> 'Yes, but while they're learning –'
>
> 'The motor's come to stay,' he answered. 'One must get about. There's a pretty church – oh, you aren't sharp enough. Well, look out, if the road worries you – right outward at the scenery.' (Ch. 23)

When they reach their destination, Margaret can hardly believe it and remarks, 'In years ago it seemed so far away'. Forster's light ironic touch, his economical narrative and realistic dialogue, accommodate a good many telling details: Margaret's humanitarian concern, Wilcox's indifference, the 'pretty church' that flashes past in an instant, the scenery that, instead of being a delight to the eye, 'heaved and merged like porridge', the modification of the sense of distance (now carried much further by jet-travel and space-travel). But Wilcox, as we now know, was right: the motor *had* come to stay, and Forster is one of the first imaginative writers to forecast its effect upon the environment and human consciousness.

This use of the motor-car has been dwelt on because it seems a particularly good instance of the integration of local realistic detail with long-term symbolic purpose – on both planes it works with complete success – and because this kind of integration is one of Forster's distinctive strengths as a novelist. It resembles his use of the 'symbolic moment' discussed earlier, in that both devices afford, as it were, a glimpse, through a crack in the surface of the everyday and the contingent, of something of much greater significance that lies beyond. They differ in that the 'symbolic moment' represents a direct challenge to the *character*, who is confronted with a choice and a parting of the moral ways, whereas the kind of example just given invites the *reader* to interpret it with reference to a wider context.

To return to the early pages of the novel: within a few chapters the contrast between the two families has been firmly established, and at the same time the ambivalent nature of the feelings with which the Schlegel sisters will come to regard the Wilcoxes has already been suggested. Helen, we are told at the beginning of Chapter 4, has 'fallen in love, not with an individual, but with a family. . . . The energy of the Wilcoxes has fascinated her'. The key word is 'energy': the Wilcox men are bossy, arrogant, insensitive, self-satisfied, philistine – and these are faults familiar to the reader of Forster, who has depicted them already in the world of the Herritons and the Pembrokes. Now, however, the picture is less one-sided and partisan: it is the Wilcoxes who, by their drive and ambition, not only make the country prosperous but make it possible for the Schlegels to draw their dividends and lead their privileged lives; so that, though not cultured themselves, they can be said to make possible the life of culture, at least for a minority. The assumption here, of course, is that personal cultivation depends on a private income. Forster evidently thinks it does and the subsequent case-history of Leonard Bast serves only to confirm his viewpoint. Others may disagree, may find a wealth of historical instances from Dr Johnson to D. H. Lawrence that disprove it, and may decide to regard this as another instance of a kind of socio-cultural tunnel-vision on Forster's part.

Later in the novel, he indirectly touches on the question again: when a group of youths are mildly disrespectful to Henry Wilcox as he walks with Margaret at the seaside (Ch. 20), Henry remarks sharply, 'And these are the men to whom we give the vote' – whereupon the narrator adds, also with a touch of Wilcoxian sharpness, 'omitting to add that they were also the men to whom he gave work as clerks – work that scarcely encouraged them to grow into other men'. Forster's thinking here seems, to use his own favourite word, a little muddled: would it have been better for the men to be unemployed? They could hardly be employed as, say, engineers if they were qualified only to be clerks; clerical work, tedious though it may be, has to be done and it seems defeatist and also unrealistic to conclude that a narrow and monotonous job precludes all possibilities of personal growth.

It may be objected then, that Forster, speaking from the limitations of his own experience and class, had an inadequate sense of the social and human realities and that he exaggerates the extent to which a truly civilised life is dependent upon an unearned income. Even in the nineteenth century, after all, the mechanics' institutes and adult schools, and the public libraries, had increased the working man's access to knowledge and culture; such landmarks as the 1896 Act of Parliament providing for the Sunday opening of museums, and the founding in 1899 of Ruskin College, Oxford, specifically for working men, were signs of the times, and there are on record many individuals whose lives are not merely success stories in the material sense but who, largely self-educated and self-motivated, acquired tastes hardly inferior to those of the Schlegels in fineness or genuineness. It is hard to believe that in his years of involvement with the Working Men's College (see p. 7) Forster had not encountered such individuals. At the same time, as Hardy's last novel, *Jude the Obscure* (1895), had graphically shown a few years earlier, it was very much more difficult for such a goal to be accomplished than it later became and it is only fair to Forster to recall that in Leonard Bast he has given a reasonably full, if not fully sympathetic, portrait of such an attempt, even though it is an attempt that fails.

Back in London, and back to Chapter 5, we find the Schlegels attending a symphony concert. The chapter contains one of Forster's most famous passages, his account of the third movement of Beethoven's Fifth Symphony, with its evocation of malign 'goblins' who 'merely observed in passing that there was no such thing as splendour or heroism in the world' and convey a message of 'panic and emptiness'. Through the music Helen is afforded a glimpse of the ultimate truth about life and its possibilities: a glimpse that comes to her not through language and reason but through what Forster elsewhere calls 'the purest of the arts'. The 'splendour of life' is real enough – but the 'goblins' are real too, even though 'men like the Wilcoxes, or President [Theodore] Roosevelt' might deny it. (The phrase again aligns the pragmatic world of business and politics in opposition to the world of art and culture, with a clear indication that truth and reality belong to the latter.)

Leaving the concert-hall precipitately at the end of the work, Helen takes with her the wrong umbrella, and in this way Leonard Bast, an impoverished, half-educated, twenty-year-old clerk with aspirations to a life of culture, enters the lives of the Schlegels. The umbrella becomes a semi-comic symbol of his precarious claim to middle-class status: his occupation and income place him in the very lowest reaches of that very broad class ('at the extreme verge of gentility' is Forster's phrase). He is genuinely upset by the loss of his umbrella, which not only deprives him, symbolically, of part of his identity but, quite realistically, is something he can ill afford to replace. Chapter 6 shows Leonard at home and represents something new in Forster's work. After deliberating quite seriously whether to spend a penny on a tramfare or to walk, he returns home to 'what is known to house-agents as a semi-basement, and to other men as a cellar', where he settles down to read Ruskin's *Stones of Venice*:

> Leonard listened to it with reverence. He felt that he was being done good to, and that if he kept on with Ruskin, and the Queen's Hall concerts, and some pictures by Watts, he would one day push his head out of the gray waters and see the universe.

Such a longing elicits a mixed response from the reader: both comic and pathetic in its conviction that a smattering of culture can confer wisdom and transform the world, it ought at the same time to command our respect and our sympathy. Forster seems to feel the absurdity more strongly than the respect, and brings out the irony and incongruity of this down-at-heel young man reading Ruskin's gorgeous prose in a cellar (Ruskin, we recall, enjoyed a private income).

Leonard's reading is interrupted by the arrival of Jacky, 'a massive woman of thirty-three' with whom he is living and whom he has promised to marry when he is 'of age' (twenty-one). Jacky's vulgarity and empty-headedness are unsparingly depicted (in Chapter 26 Forster describes her as 'bestially stupid') and few of Forster's critics have had a good word to say for her; indeed, the whole of the Leonard–Jacky portion of the novel, which may be regarded as a subplot, has usually been judged a weakness or even dismissed as a total failure. Leavis describes these two characters as 'a mere external grasping at something that lies outside the author's first-hand experience', and it is true that the description of their home life, and the dialogue put into their mouths, carry little conviction and remind us that, compared with novelists such as Dickens or D. H. Lawrence, Forster's own intimate knowledge of English society was very restricted. At the same time he does go a little way towards conveying something of the pathos of Leonard's situation: not so much his poverty, a theme which other novelists such as Gissing had already treated much more fully and authoritatively, as his eager but inevitably frustrated yearning after the life of the mind.

It is, however, only a very little way, and Forster does not really pay the respect that is due to Leonard's clumsy, fumbling attempts to fertilise his arid existence with Beethoven and Ruskin. There is a failure to tone that proceeds from a fundamental lack of sympathy, and Leonard's efforts are too often presented in a comic or ironic light. A damaging result of this is that when Leonard is later called upon to sustain an important and serious role in the unfolding of the plot he is not really adequate to this function: the reader, having accepted him as a kind of Mr Polly, finds it difficult to adjust to a view of him as a tragic figure. Forster treats Leonard not as an individual but as a 'case'. As such he assumes some importance, notably when Margaret uses him to reproach Henry Wilcox with a heartless lack of social responsibility; but when presenting

Leonard in close-up Forster is still enslaved by the nineteenth-century convention that makes it difficult for lower-class speech to be compatible with anything but 'comic relief'.

Still, for all its artistic imperfections this element of the novel does seem to convey an uneasiness on Forster's part: if, as he reflects, 'Some are born cultured' and the rest had better not engage in the impossible struggle to acquire culture, this seems to be a sad denial of the democratic spirit that judges men by intrinsic worth and not by class or income, and that Forster elsewhere passionately urges. Again we are made aware of the limitations of Forster's social vision: Leonard is not only culturally underprivileged but actually undernourished: his real-life counterparts would have been among those who were found unfit for active service in 1914. Yet his economic plight, the plight of his whole class and of the millions below him in the social hierarchy, is scarcely touched on except as a stick to beat Henry Wilcox. At the beginning of the chapter describing Leonard's home life. Forster has blandly declared, 'We are not concerned with the very poor': while he is as a novelist entitled to confine his attention to any social group he cares to select, he seems to have placed himself in the somewhat unsatisfactory position of raising issues (e.g. Leonard's starvation-level employment and the Schlegel sisters' guilt-feeling about their unearned income) and then failing to pursue them with thoroughness and seriousness to their conclusion.

After Leonard, acting on Henry's advice, has given up his job for one even less well-paid, the advice turns out to be unsound; and this leads, in Chapter 22, to a major scene between Henry and Margaret in which he (like Herbert Pembroke in *The Longest Journey*) resorts to clichés such as 'the battle of life' and 'all in the day's work', and insists that 'No one's to blame', while Margaret is determined to make him see, and feel, his moral responsibility. What she tries, in vain, to make him do is to 'connect', to have a sense of obligations that override class barriers and legal duties. But again there is a sense that Leonard's is not a fully realised individual tragedy but only a convenient occasion for the debate between two well-defined value-systems: humanistic concern and capitalistic indifference. (An instructive contrast may be made with Dickens's treatment of a similar theme half a century earlier in

Hard Times (1854), and Mrs Gaskell's in *North and South* (1855); probably coincidentally, the heroine of the latter is another Margaret.)

The involvement of Leonard with the Schlegels and the Wilcoxes comes to a head in Chapter 26 when Helen, refusing to compromise her idealism as her sister has done, brings Leonard and Jacky into the Wilcox circle. Leonard, now jobless and penniless, is by Helen's account 'starving' and by his own about to 'fall over the edge' into the abyss of poverty and degradation. When Jacky and Henry come face to face by accident, it emerges that she had been his mistress ten years earlier. He assumes that the exposure has been planned by Margaret, but the encounter is merely the result of a fairly considerable coincidence – one that comes in a little too pat, underlining as it does the responsibility than Henry has shrugged off but now has a directly personal motive for feeling.

By this time Margaret has become engaged to Henry, and we need to go back to a somewhat earlier stage of the novel in order to consider this crucial development. The main plot of the novel concerns the way in which the two families become connected by two different means. One of them relates to the house, Howards End: when Mrs Wilcox dies suddenly (yet another of Forster's deaths-without-warning: Chapter 11 begins, 'The funeral was over . . .') it turns out that she had intended the house to go to Margaret, in whom, despite their very slight acquaintance, she had recognised a kindred spirit. However, her family persuade themselves that her wish need not be taken seriously and Margaret learns nothing about it until the last page of the novel. As the narrator points out:

> To them Howards End was a house: they could not know that to her it had been a spirit, for which she sought a spiritual heir. (Ch. 11)

The bequest had been symbolic or sacramental, but this is a language or level of meaning unintelligible to the Wilcoxes, who see the house not in a 'spiritual' light but as bricks and mortar, valuable and saleable. There is an effective irony in Margaret's delight and gratitude that she has been given (a sop to the family conscience) Mrs Wilcox's 'silver vinaigrette', and the whole transaction recalls the somewhat similar behaviour of the Dashwoods in the second chapter of Jane Austen's *Sense and Sensibility*.

In the long run, Mrs Wilcox's dying wish is belatedly fulfilled and the house passes to the Schlegels in the closing pages of the book. But this connection between the two families is, so to speak, subterranean or hidden from some of those most nearly concerned. A more visible and public connection is established through the marriage of Margaret and Henry. Forster's symbolic or allegorical purpose seems reasonably clear: if the Wilcoxes of this world need an infusion of Schlegel culture and morality, the Schlegels no less need to acquire the Wilcox energy and effectiveness in the practical sphere (the effete Tibby illustrating the dire effects of its absence), and the marriage represents a blending of the strengths of both. But many readers have been unwilling to accept Margaret's action as psychologically plausible: as so often in Forster, the plot seems to take a sudden lurch forward, or turns a corner unexpectedly, with inadequate explanation and even in a manner that may seem wildly improbable. What Forster refers to as Henry's 'masterly ways' must probably be seen as having a strong attraction for Margaret, but Forster hardly begins to explore (as Lawrence, for instance, might have done) the sexual power of a man of Henry's type. The important thing to note, however, is that Margaret does not abandon her principles after her engagement and marriage: the second Mrs Wilcox remains a Schlegel at heart if not in law, and her ultimate achievement is nothing less than the salvation of her husband, though external circumstances come dramatically, and even melodramatically, to her aid in order that this may be accomplished.

Two dramatic episodes show that Margaret is still her own woman. In the first (Ch. 25), she impulsively jumps out of a moving car when Charles Wilcox has refused to go back after running over a cat. In spite of assurances that the 'Men will see to it' and that the cat's owner, a cottage-dweller, will be quickly consoled by some small financial compensation, she insists on seeing the small event as a moral issue and one that she is personally involved in and cannot leave to others. In behaving thus unconventionally and indecorously, that is, she is behaving exactly in accordance with Forster's convictions as to what constitutes right conduct – that conduct which, according to

Matthew Arnold, is three-quarters of life. The episode is a telling one, though the moralising narrator, as often in Forster, goes a little too far in his condemnation of the Wilcoxes' spiritual emptiness: 'They had no part with the earth and its emotions. They were dust, and a stink, and cosmopolitan chatter, and the girl whose cat had been killed had lived more deeply than they.' Although presented as Margaret's reflections, these are plainly endorsed by the narrator, and there is perhaps a touch of sentimentality and inverted class-consciousness in the facile assumption that the girl who 'screamed wildly at them' was prompted by intense feeling, just as there is something odd in the half-German Margaret's thinking of the jingoistic Wilcoxes as 'cosmopolitan'.

The second episode has been prepared for by a sequence of events: Helen has disappeared for a time but has at last been, in effect, ambushed at Howards End, where her sister discovers that she is pregnant and has been keeping out of the way in order to conceal her condition. The child is Leonard's, Helen having given herself to him in a quixotic and almost symbolic gesture that, like many of Forster's symbolic gestures, does not quite work on the level of realism. Needless to say, the precise circumstances of the sexual encounter are glossed over – a feature that prompted Katherine Mansfield to note sardonically in her journal (May 1917) that she could 'never be perfectly certain whether Helen was got with child by Leonard Bast or by his fatal forgotten umbrella. All things considered, I think it must have been the umbrella.' (Compare her comment, in a review three years later [*Athenaeum*, 13 August 1920], on Forster's 'extreme reluctance to – shall we say? – commit himself wholly.')

In Chapter 38, in one of the best scenes in the novel, Henry refuses to allow Helen to spend the night in the house: assuming a strict and unforgiving moral attitude, he seems to believe (or to affect to believe) that her presence would be a kind of moral pollution, and he once more falls back on clichés ('false to my position in society', 'the memory of my dear wife to consider') to bolster a stance unsupported by any real moral conviction. Goaded by his sanctimonious reference to his dead wife, Margaret forces him to see 'the connection':

'Not any more of this!' she cried. 'You shall see the connection if it kills you, Henry! You have had a mistress – I forgave you. My sister has a lover – you drive her from the house. Do you see the connection?'

But – and here Forster resists novelistic banality and is courageously true to life – Henry is unmoved, accuses her of attempting to blackmail him, and repeats his prohibition.

The underlying moral and dramatic pattern of the novel should now be clear. The ways of life, and of thinking and feeling, that the two families embody are subjected to a series of tests: one is provided by Leonard Bast, another by Mrs Wilcox's wishes regarding Howards End, yet another by Helen's pregnancy (these being, of course, not separate elements but closely connected). By stages, the shallowness, human inadequacy, hypocrisy and self-deception of the Wilcoxes are exposed: they live by catchwords and unquestioned rules of thumb rather than genuinely responding to a particular moral issue.

So far so good: but Forster, like all novelists, has the problem of bringing his book to a conclusion. Even though Rex Warner has suggested that 'the book's value is in the definition rather than in the solution of a problem',[55] end it must: as we have seen already, endings always gave Forster trouble and the manuscript of *Howards End* furnishes evidence of a 'startling . . . uncertainty of aim' (the phrase is Oliver Stallybrass's). Forster's working notes show that he toyed with various possibilities:

> Then I think that Charles . . . is sent by his father to horse whip Leonard, and is killed by him, and L flings himself out of the window.
> Or it may be that Helen & Leonard die.
> Or perhaps Leonard lives.[56]

In the event, he resolved this dithering by resorting to an ending remarkably similar to that of *The Longest Journey*: there is sudden and violent death in symbolic circumstances (Ch. 41), and a pastoral coda, also fraught with symbolism, in which a child offers a promise of the future and the theme of inheritance – spiritual rather than material – is prominent, the whole adding up to a mood of reconciliation and optimism that Leavis judges to be 'in its innocent way, sentimental'. Leonard, who had perhaps always been a slight embarrassment to his creator, is dispatched from the scene by a convenient heart-attack, and this also neatly effects the punishment of Charles Wilcox and the moral regeneration of his father, who is (as he puts it in Chapter 43) 'broken' and 'ended' by his son's disgrace and imprisonment. Whether, in the nature of the case, any court would have handed down such a sentence may be questioned, and there is something glib and facile about Forster's perfunctory handling of the matter: 'It was against all reason that he should be punished, but the law, being made in his image, sentenced him to three years' imprisonment.' Charles must go to prison, however, not because, in realistic terms, this is how society necessarily works but because his father must be utterly crushed as the first stage of his rebirth into a new life: 'Then Henry's fortress gave away. He could bear no one but his wife, he shambled up to Margaret afterwards and asked her to do what she could with him.' It is hard to believe that this is how the Henry Wilcox we have come to know during the previous three hundred pages would have responded; and what we have is, in fact, a version of a device beloved by nineteenth-century novelists (the long tradition extending from, for example, Tom Bertram in *Mansfield Park* to Angel Clare in *Tess of the d'Urbervilles*): the physical or mental crisis, usually a dangerous illness, that purges a character of baser elements and enables him to see the world with new eyes.

Forster's placing of the name of the house in the final phrase of this penultimate chapter is no accident (five words that originally followed it in the manuscript were deleted); and the epilogue-like Chapter 44 returns not only to the house but to the hay-symbolism associated from the first with Mrs Wilcox, who now seems to hover over the scene like an affable familiar ghost. A year or more has passed, and Helen's baby is almost able to stand, but Henry remains 'shut up in the house', plagued by hayfever, and when he speaks it is 'in a weary voice'. The hayfever suggests that he is still unregenerate – Forster, it seems, does not believe that even a repentant goat can be transformed into a sheep – but his one positive act implies repentance: he intends to leave the house to his wife when he dies, thus fulfilling his first wife's wish. For her part Margaret will bequeath it to her nephew and Leonard, surviving through his son, whom Trilling describes as 'the symbol of the classless society', will achieve vicariously a life that was denied to him in his person. The poor will inherit the earth.

The mood is not wholly serene, however, For one thing, Helen reminds her sister that 'London's creeping' – a favourite theme of Forster's. But Margaret's reply voices an optimism based on faith, or at least hope, rather than reason:

> This craze for motion has only set in during the last hundred years. It may be followed by a civilisation that won't be a movement, because it will rest on the earth.

More puzzling are Margaret's final words, spoken to her husband: 'Nothing has been done wrong'. Unless we read this as a reassurance to a half-senile man rather than a meaningful statement, it may be taken as implying a disturbing shift in the firm moral stance that Margaret has maintained throughout the book; and some have interpreted it as Forster's recognition that real life calls for compromises that may amount to a betrayal of liberal ideas. Equally, though, it can be taken as expressing a faith in meliorism – in the gradual betterment of the human condition and the inevitable victory of right.

As the foregoing commentary has suggested, *Howards End* is a novel with great strengths but equally undeniable weaknesses. As elsewhere, Forster sometimes seems to vacillate a little uncertainly between realism and allegory, to try to 'bounce' the reader into accepting psychological and practical improbabilities, and to force upon the complexities of life and personality an oversimplified moral pattern. It has, however, all the seriousness of *The Longest Journey* without (for the most part) that novel's thinness of characterisation and distressing excursions into pseudo-poetical prose.[57] Stallybrass's claim that, despite its flaws, it is of all Forster's novels 'perhaps the most quintessential'[58] carries conviction.

1. Slide
2. Lift
3. Close
4. Press

1. Slide the on-off switch to on.

5

A Passage to India

As we saw in Chapter 1, Forster visited India in 1912–13 and again in 1921. The novel that became *A Passage to India* was begun before the outbreak of war in 1914, but little progress was made, and Forster's modest involvement in wartime activities was sufficient to interrupt his career as a novelist even if there had been no other reason – no distressing 'block' – for his failure to produce a successor to *Howards End*. Back in England in 1922 after the second visit, he again took up what he was soon referring to as 'my Indian novel' (letter of 18 July 1923), and by the beginning of 1924 he was able to report, 'Now it is done and I think it good' (27 January 1924). It had not come easily: in 1922, he had made a 'sacrificial burning of a number of short stories . . . in order that a Passage to India might get finished'; this confession, in a letter of 16 January 1935, not only suggests the difficulties he had in resuming work on the novel but also the curious coexistence in his rational and sceptical temperament of a vein of superstition and belief in magic.

A Passage to India was published on 4 June 1924: Forster was forty-five years old and fourteen years had elapsed since the appearance of his previous novel. It was a popular and critical success: Philip Gardner notes that 'It was reviewed more extensively than any of its predecessors, and hardly a dissonant voice marred the equally extensive acclamation.'[59] Five days after publication, Forster reported that 'The sales have begun well', and by the end of the year he recorded that it was doing extremely well in America, with sales of 'about 30,000 and still going strong'. Some whose knowledge of India was more intimate than Forster's were quick to point out inaccuracies: it appears, for instance, that his use of the term 'Burra Sahib' is not authentic and, more seriously, that the climactic courtroom scene is flawed by his ignorance of the correct legal procedures.

No doubt the topicality of the novel contributed to its success: Rebecca West significantly described it in a review as a 'study of a certain problem of the British Empire'. It was not only topical but controversial, and in one of his letters (23 December 1924) Forster refers to the possibility that it might be banned by the British government (the short-lived Labour government had been replaced by the Conservatives in the previous month). In the closing years of the nineteenth century Kipling had opened up the subcontinent as rich fictional territory hitherto virtually unexplored and unexploited: his immensely popular stories and poems depicting the lives of Anglo-Indians were at once romantic and disturbing, and opened the eyes of readers who had never seen India to the complexity of its problems. A generation later, the problems had become more rather than less acute: though independence was still twenty years away, political agitation and even rioting indicated the strength of the demand until at last, three years after Forster's novel appeared, the Simon Commission was set up to advise on the need for change.

An important point is that the situation had already changed significantly in the years between Forster's two visits. Most notably, riots in the Punjab in 1919 had come to a head in the Amritsar massacre, when troops who had opened fire on an unarmed crowd killed 379 Indians and wounded over a thousand. It has been argued that the tone of the novel reflects the less troubled India of Forster's first visit rather than the graver situation that had emerged even before the book was completed, and that its treatment of the political and racial situation was therefore already dated on the day of publication. Any answer to this criticism must involve an insistence that the novel is not merely, or even mainly, a study of contemporary India that stands or falls by its historical authenticity. Its topicality, like that of some earlier classic novels such as Dickens's *Bleak House* and *Little Dorrit*, is combined with a vision of human life and human nature that transcends specific periods and places. As Forster himself later pointed out:

> the book is not really about politics, though it is the political aspect of it that caught the general public and made it sell. It's about something wider than politics, about the search of

the human race for a more lasting home, about the universe as embodied in the Indian earth and the horror lurking in the Marabar Caves and the release symbolized by the birth of Krishna.[60]

He goes on to explain that the intention of the novel was 'philosophic and poetic' and that for this reason he borrowed his title from a poem by Walt Whitman, the American writer whose major themes include political, spiritual and sexual freedom.

With the possible exception of *The Longest Journey*, no previous novel by Forster could be described as predominantly 'philosophic and poetic', and so the above claim may suggest a bold confrontation with new problems and even an attempt to write an entirely different kind of novel – something more closely related to the work of the great European masters such as Dostoevski and Kafka, or the experimental fiction of André Gide (whom Forster discusses in *Aspects of the Novel*), rather than to the English tradition of sociological and topographical realism. It is as well, therefore, to draw attention to the continuity of Forster's last novel with the rest of his fiction. In turning to India as a setting he was certainly doing something new, but to a large extent the themes of *Passage* are those of the earlier books. Personal relationships are still his overriding concern, though the arena is now not London or Cambridge or the Home Counties but a teeming subcontinent. Its scope and ambitiousness is suggested by the fact that whereas he had previously presented the conflict between temperaments and systems of values within a single culture – for the contrasts between English and Italians, or the philistines and the enlightened, or the upper-middle and lower-middle classes, all function within a European and mainly an Anglo-Saxon context – he now depicted different races, cultures and creeds existing in a land that is remote from Europe not only in distance but in landscape, architecture and climate. Granted this larger and more complex setting, however, it should be recognised that Forster is still exploring familiar themes. If, as is often maintained, this is his masterpiece, it is not because it represents any sudden invasion of new territory: *The Longest Journey*, for instance, though a very English novel, anticipates to some extent the philosophical or metaphysical quest, the 'something wider than politics', of the later novel, which in its turn is much concerned with the exploration of social and sexual relationships in a familiar vein of ironic comedy. And earlier character-types have a way of reappearing in this Indian novel: Ronny Heaslop is a reworking of the public-school type now filling the role of a pukka sahib, and Turton resembles Herbert Pembroke in a solar topee.

Structurally, again, the *Passage* bears a marked resemblance to some of its predecessors. The three-part division of *The Longest Journey* is used once more, and as in that novel each part is named after a place and each place associated not only with a group of characters but with a way of life and set of values. But here too the *scale* on which Forster is now operating is almost breathtakingly larger. Whereas, for instance, the differences between Cambridge and Sawston are differences within a narrow social and geographical segment of English society – for, despite their sharply opposed value-systems, the representatives of Cambridge and Sawston are all English, white, protestant and middle class – the contrasts are now between those of different races and religions. In the three parts of *Passage*, 'Mosque' emphasises the Moslem world of Aziz and his friends, 'Caves' the British or Anglo-Indian element, and 'Temple' the Hindu. These are, of course, only emphases, and the real preoccupation of the book is with the collision between rather than the separate identify of races and religions, but the division draws attention at once to the diversity and complexity of India and its problems.

It is natural to ask how successfully Forster rises to the demands of such a theme, the most ambitious he had ever undertaken. When we turn to the first page of the novel, we find no loftiness of language, no suggestion that he is striving for a high seriousness hitherto absent from his art: on the contrary, there is an element of deflation, of playing down any possible glamour and picturesqueness that might seem to belong to the fictitious town of Chandrapore. From the first sentence onwards ('nothing extraordinary'), negatives cluster in the opening paragraph: it is almost as though Forster were reversing, and hence exposing the hollowness of, the too-enthusiastic style of guide-books or passing tourists: 'The streets are mean, the temples ineffective. . .'. There is a characteristic use of the barbed colloquialism in the observation that 'the Ganges happens not to be holy here'. And yet it should not be overlooked that this is after all an opening quite different from those of the earlier novels. Forster's habitual way of beginning is to depict, with minimal preliminaries, a *social* scene often quite trivial or commonplace in itself (the station platform in *Where Angels*, the undergraduate discussion in *The Longest Journey*) but which touches unobtrusively on some of the themes, and introduces some of the characters, of the story. What is exceptional in *Passage* is than mankind is almost absent from the opening chapter, which concerns itself with the visible scene.

The structure of the short opening chapter has a symmetry that suggests a concern on Forster's part with form and pattern – or, to employ the term he used shortly afterwards in *Aspects of the Novel*, with 'rhythm'. Of the chapter's four paragraphs, the first two describe the earth, the last two the sky. (The words 'earth' and 'sky' are to recur, not accidentally, in the final paragraph of the novel.) Between the first two paragraphs there is a further contrast: while the native part of the city, straggling along the rubbish-strewn banks of the river, seems ready to sink into the primeval mud from which it originally emerged ('The very wood seems made of mud, the inhabitants of mud moving'), the homes of the Eurasians and the civil station occupied by the British stand on higher ground. It is, in other words, a city of sharp geographical divisions that correspond to racial differences. But above them all, as Forster tells us at the end of the second paragraph – and the phrase, thus prominently placed, introduces the contrasting second half of the chapter – is 'the overarching sky'. In these closing paragraphs Forster's style undergoes a marked change: the somewhat dry, detached, even colloquial tone of the opening gives way to a more poetic use of language ('the stars hang like lamps from the immense vault'); the 'rubbish', 'filth' and 'mud' of the townscape are replaced by brilliant colours (orange, purple, blue); negatives are replaced by positive assertions ('The sky settles everything. . .'). Finally, the symmetry of the chapter is completed by its last word, 'caves', which echoes the first noun of the opening sentence as the caves themselves are later to send forth echoes.

Already Forster has done a good deal, sounding the themes of separation and difference, of the possibility of unity (the 'overarching sky' embracing all, like the symbolic rainbow of Lawrence's novel only nine years earlier, and recalling the 'only connect' of *Howards End*), and stressing, unobtrusively but surely, the presence of the caves that are to be so important in both the action and the symbolic pattern of the novel. If this opening chapter looks at first glance like 'description' or 'setting the scene', this can be only a very superficial impression: it is that, but a great deal more besides, and even apparently casual details form part of a subtle design (note, for instance, the references to the roads in the civil station intersecting 'at right angles', the native quarter of Chandrapore following the course of the river, the 'curve' of the earth and the 'vault' and 'dome' of the sky). Forster is not giving us 'background' but something much more like the overture to an opera (we recall that he was a lifelong lover of music), in which themes and motifs to be developed later are hinted at within a structure that has its own formal design and unity.

In comparison with the openings of Forster's earlier novels, that of *Passage* has an exceptional seriousness and deliberation: the casualness, almost offhandedness, and the comedy have yielded to an ambitious, even portentous poetic treatment; the characters are no longer confined to the English bourgeoisie but are races, humanity in the mass, and even the earth and the sky; the field of reference is no longer merely social but cosmic. For a parallel we have to turn to Hardy's *The Return of the Native*, and like that novel *Passage* moves in its second chapter to the world of human action; but (as with Hardy) the formal and aesthetic point has been made – this is to be a novel in which structure, pattern and rhythm will count for a good deal. One simple but striking piece of evidence of this concern with shape and form – fictional qualities that were, again, to receive attention in Forster's 1927 lectures, where, for example, he compares the shape of one of Anatole France's novels to that of an hourglass – is the placing of the Marabar Caves incident exactly in the middle of the book. The centre-point of a text traditionally enjoyed special and almost magical status (Crusoe's discovery of the footprint in the sand in Defoe's novel is a famous case in point), and it can hardly be coincidental that Forster has placed this episode, so crucial to theme and plot, in that position. What follows from this emphasis on form and pattern is that the reader must be sensitive to repetitions and parallels – echoes, one might say – and agile in making connections between different parts of the novel, sometimes on the basis of tiny clues.[61]

Let us look in more detail at the structuring of the novel's three parts. The first, 'Mosque', contains eleven chapters, of which the first has already been discussed. The second introduces Aziz, who is a doctor, a widower and a Muslim: first at a dinner-party among his friends, at which they discuss the question (which the novel itself is to explore more exhaustively) 'whether or no it is possible to be friends with an Englishman'; then receiving 'the inevitable snub' from Major Callender, the Anglo-Indian Civil Surgeon who is his professional superior, and Mrs Callender; and thirdly in his encounter in the mosque at night with Mrs Moore, who has recently arrived from England to visit her son, Ronny Heaslop, who is the City Magistrate. In Chapter 3 Angela Quested appears: she is a 'queer, cautious girl' who is engaged to Ronny and has come out from England with Mrs Moore to see India and the new life that awaits her when, or if, she marries him. Fielding, the schoolmaster at the Government College, also appears and laconically advises the newcomers that the best way of seeing 'the real India' is to 'Try seeing Indians'. Chapters 4 and 5 describe the 'Bridge Party', a contrived and unsuccessful official attempt to bring together educated Indians and Anglo-Indian officials and their wives on a formal social occasion – an attempt without any genuine human impulse behind it; Chapter 5 ends with an argument between Ronny and his mother concerning the role of the British in India. Chapter 6 returns to Aziz, who receives an invitation from Fielding, and the next chapter presents Fielding more fully than hitherto and shows the development of his relationship with Aziz; at 'an "unconventional" party' the latter meets Miss Quested and (again) Mrs Moore and impulsively invites them to visit the Marabar Caves as his guests. Professor Godbole, a Brahmin, also appears in this long chapter, but the party turns sour on the appearance of Ronny, who takes exception to the growing friendships between British and Indians.

The proposed visit to the caves polarises the British. Ronny is against it, and interprets it as a crafty plot on the part of Aziz to enhance his own status (an uncharitable and wholly erroneous view); Fielding is for it, as a means of promoting Anglo-Indian

relationships. Fielding emerges in this chapter as 'a disruptive
force' who has excited the disapproval of his fellow-countrymen
by trying to form friendships with Indians: one of the weaknesses
of the David Lean film of *A Passage to India* lies in its depiction
of Fielding as a suave and amiable rather than as a somewhat
defiantly nonconformist character. Adela, unaware of the
complex issues raised in India by even such an apparently
simple matter as an invitation to a picnic, feels the naïve
enthusiasm of a tourist and a somewhat prim pride in doing
what she senses is daringly unorthodox. Like Lucy Honeychurch
in *A Room with a View*, she is an innocent abroad, though later
Forster is to stress her stupidity and commonplaceness more
insistently than he does with his earlier heroine.

In Chapter 8, Adela first breaks off her engagement to Ronny
and then renews it; when Mrs Moore is told that they intend to
be married, she resolves privately that, her reason for coming to
India having been fulfilled, she can now go home. Chapter 9
returns to Aziz and his friends; Aziz is ill, Fielding visits him in
his rather squalid home, and they discuss the presence of the
British in India. Chapter 10 is very short – even shorter than
Chapter 1 – and like Chapter 1 it steps back from the human
scene and evokes a world in which the forces of nature, and
especially the sun, are dominant and render human decision
and human action trivial by comparison. As Ronny remarks in
Chapter 5, 'There's nothing in India but the weather', and the
two paragraphs of Chapter 10 remind us that 'April, herald of
horrors, is at hand' and that 'The sun was returning to his
kingdom with power but without beauty – that was the sinister
feature': the cruel sun of the tropics, that is, not the welcome
sun of the temperate zones. Chapter 11, which concludes Part
I, shows the further development of the relationship between
the Englishman and the Indian, Fielding and Aziz, which is a
main axis of the novel. In a symbolic act expressing his trust
and desire for 'brotherhood', Aziz shows the other man a
photograph of his dead wife and (unconsciously echoing an
earlier speech by Mrs Moore) tells him that 'Kindness, more
kindness, and even after that more kindness' is needed between
the races who live together, yet apart, in India.

If we pause at this point to consider what *kind* of novel
Forster has given us in the first part (slightly more than one-
third of the whole), it may seem to be little more than a

familiar mixture. His characters are almost exclusively middle-
class (civil servants, doctors, teachers, ladies of leisure). As for
his mode of story-telling, he proceeds by a series of encounters
on a variety of social occasions largely narrated through
dramatic dialogue: Mrs Moore meets Aziz, Ronny argues with
Adela and his mother, Fielding talks to Aziz, and so forth. The
possibilities of different combinations and contrasts are considerable, but the actual number of characters is in fact quite
small – no more than half-a-dozen or so major characters,
with a further handful of minor figures. The larger scenes, such
as the bridge party in Chapter 5 and Fielding's tea-party in
Chapter 7, recall the balls and dinners of a Jane Austen novel;
indeed the technique of *Passage* seems to have much in common
with that of Forster's earlier novels and of a strong tradition in
nineteeth-century realistic fiction.

To suggest this, and to argue that Forster is after all doing
nothing very new, is, however, to overlook some important
elements. One is the scale and complexity of the novel's fictional
world. Jane Austen had in a famous phrase recommended
'three or four families in a country village' as sufficient material
for the novelist, and George Eliot in her finest novel had limited
her attention to a single Midlands town, but Forster's character-
groups straddle continents, races and religions. The collisions,
misunderstandings and struggles for friendship and love are
now not (or not only) between classes and temperaments but
between larger and even more radically divided societies whose
members have different customs and values, enjoy different
political status, and literally speak different languages. There is
an unobtrusive but significant exchange in Chapter 7 when,
responding to Adela's announcement that she hates mysteries,
Mrs Moore tells her that she herself likes mysteries but dislikes
muddles. Adela's blithe and typically shallow insistence that
they are the same thing does not carry conviction. 'Muddle' is,
as we have seen already, one of Forster's favourite words, and
his plots and incidents often turn upon 'muddles'. But with a
few isolated exceptions – Gino bathing the baby in *Where Angels
Fear to Tread*, some passages (especially those concerned with
Stephen) in *The Longest Journey*, the description of Beethoven's
Fifth Symphony in *Howards End* – there is not a great deal of
'mystery' in Forster's previous novels (the short stories are
another matter, though the 'mystery' there is often of a

decidedly arch and factitious kind and is allied with the supernatural and the mythological). Now, in *Passage*, 'mystery' occupies the heart of the novel, and Forster's assurance that he understands and can explain both what people do and what they ought to do deserts him at crucial moments. India may be, as he says, a muddle, and this is depicted in his familiar ironic manner, but it is also a mystery, and the presence of something transcending social relationships is signalled by the short but potent first and tenth chapters. In a limited sense, it is true, *Passage* is, like *Howards End* or *Pride and Prejudice*, a 'marriage novel', and the question whether Adela will after all marry Ronny is part of the plot-interest; but such issues pale into significance beneath the overarching sky and the burning sun of whose presence we are made aware. *Passage* is a novel about love, but ultimately the kind of love that finds fulfilment in the institution of marriage is seen to be trivial in relation to the possibility of a deep and abiding relationship between the members of different races, and of love – or the absence of it – as a guiding principle of the universe. The only marriage of true minds that really interests Forster in this novel is the one that is seen as possible, though it remains unfulfilled at the end, between Aziz and Fielding.

Not surprisingly, part of Forster's reaction to India had been a social reaction: with such a keen observer it could hardly have been otherwise, and his notations began before he ever set foot there, for in a letter written on his way out in October 1912 he is already registering his reaction to Anglo-Indians in terms crude and undeveloped in themselves but not fundamentally different from those of the novel: 'The women are pretty rotten, & vile on the native question: their husbands better.'[62] But when he came to write the novel he placed the analysis and criticism of a society within a larger framework that it is not unduly pretentious to describe as philosophical or metaphysical, as if a novel by Jane Austen had become embedded in one by Albert Camus or William Golding. Without quitting the English tradition of realism and even of social satire and domestic comedy, Forster moves in his last novel beyond that tradition to examine, as Dostoevski and Kafka do, the nature of man and of the universe.

In stressing the novel's larger scope, however, we ought not to play down the complexity and effectiveness of its social

aspects. As the outline of Part I already given has suggested,
Forster depicts and develops an unprecedentedly wide range of
relationships in which the variables are race, colour, political
status and religion as well as class, sex, occupation, marital
status, temperament and values. The most important contrasting
groups, British and Indian, quickly subdivide: the British
include Anglo-Indians or those who have made their lives and
careers in the country (Heaslop, Fielding, Callender), and those
who, like Mrs Moore, see it as outsiders. (Adela is a member of
the second category who must decide whether she wants to join
the first.) The Indians include Muslims (Aziz and his friends)
and Hindus (Godbole). But the most significant members of
the groups are those who wish to cross the lines of division,
especially the central quartet of Adela, Mrs Moore, Fielding
and Aziz. These make their not always consistent efforts to
break down barriers against a background of those, both British
and Indian, who believe that the two races can never come
together in friendship. As the novel proceeds, the real possibility
of contact comes to be restricted to the relationship between
Aziz and Fielding – a symptom, perhaps, of Forster's limited
capacity to deal at all adequately with women characters, and
indeed his lack of interest in attempting to do so.

But this is to anticipate, and an account of the second and
third parts of the novel will now be in order. As Colmer has
said: 'Each of the three main parts, Mosque, Caves, and
Temple, has a theme, a tone, an atmosphere of its own, while
contributing to the total structure of the novel.'[63] The idea of
the mosque has featured in the first part not only in the
prominence given to the Muslim Aziz but also, quite literally,
as the building in which, in the cool open air and significantly
apart from the hot and hearty jollity of the British, Aziz and
Mrs Moore have encountered each other for the first time. Part
II is dominated by the Marabar Caves, and although Aziz
continues to be a focus of attention, we are now given a fuller
account of British rule as exemplified in the official as well as
the private reaction to Adela's allegations. Like Part I, it
begins with the land: before humanity comes geology, with the
land rising from the ocean, the gods taking their seats on the
mountains and 'contriving' the holy river of the Ganges. It is as
though Forster were rewriting in acceptable twentieth-century
terms the opening verses of Genesis: the 'high places of Dravidia'

are 'older than anything in the world', and the dark and womb-like Marabar Caves which they contain may be expected to hold, if anywhere does, the secret of existence.

From this evocation of geological time and this metaphysical speculation in Chapter 12, Chapter 13 descends promptly to the contemporary social reality. The preparations for the visit, and the departure, involve a comedy of confusions and embarrassments, an amusing muddle that only later on turns out to be capable of sinister interpretation. The accident whereby Fielding and Godbole are left behind and Aziz becomes responsible for the welfare of the English ladies, with a chance to prove the unsoundness of the Anglo-Indian adage that 'Indians are incapable of responsibility', is soon put aside. Forster's handling of the early stages of the central and crucial episode is resolutely comic: Aziz leaps on to the moving train, the servant emerges from the lavatory 'with tea and poached eggs upon a tray', an elephant awaits their arrival (a brilliant stroke of hospitality that makes Aziz 'nearly burst with pride and relief'). The dialogue is brisk and natural, with much banter and some feigned enthusiasm of a highly conventional kind, and there are touches of realistic comic detail such as the vase of artificial flowers that stands in the centre of the cloth spread for an outdoor meal. All this is the context or setting for what is to become within a few pages Forster's most celebrated incursion into poetic symbolism and metaphysical suggestion.

As they refresh themselves before entering the cave, the party talk, and Adela tells Aziz of her forthcoming marriage, which will inevitably ally her with the Anglo-Indians. But while being unable to 'avoid the label' of Anglo-Indian, she hopes (she tells him) to 'avoid . . . the mentality', and she asks him for advice. For a moment the two races draw closer, in a civilised intimacy of equals; there have already been other such moments between Aziz and Fielding and between Aziz and Mrs Moore, and they are moments that show the possibility of a loving kindness that transcends the barriers of race. Aziz, however, is angered by her sad comment that she has been 'told we all get rude [to Indians] after a year' – angered because he recognises its truth – and the intimacy is shattered. It is at this point, with Adela's mind full of thoughts of her marriage and its distasteful consequences, that they enter the caves.

Mrs Moore's experience there is distressing: the pressure and smell of bodies (for they are accompanied by a crowd of Indians) cause her to be overcome by faintness and claustrophobic panic, she bangs her head, and she is terrified by the echo. Though she apparentlly soon recovers when she is again in the open air, she has had enough of caves and decides to sightsee no more. This is the latest in a series of accidents that, as it later turns out, collectively conspire against Aziz: Fielding and Godbole have missed the train, Ronny's servant Antony has been bribed to stay behind, now Mrs Moore's fatigue ensures that Adela will be unchaperoned.

As it turns out, Mrs Moore suffers from something worse than fatigue: the more she thinks about her experience in the cave, 'the more disagreeable and frightening it became', and she feels progressively 'despair', terror and 'horror' (this last noun bringing to mind the experience of another European in the tropics, Conrad's Kurtz in *Heart of Darkness*, who had also been appalled by a revelation of the emptiness and meaninglessness of life). Her feelings are particularly connected with the echo in the cave, the 'boum' into which every sound, trivial or profound, is converted. For her the message of the echo is that 'Everything exists, nothing has value' and the foundations on which her life has rested, from personal relationships to Christian faith, seem to be slipping away beneath her. The experience changes her permanently: her concern for other people fades into boredom and indifference, her earlier life seems like a dream, and she displays only irritation and impatience with the small matters that make up most of human life. After the glimpse into the abyss, nothing seems to matter, and from this point she retreats from the social scene and from life itself, so that when it comes, her death seems inevitable.

There is a sharp transition in tone from the end of Chapter 14, with its account of Mrs Moore 'motionless with horror' and abandoning rational explanations in her surrender to the pessimistic, life-denying 'vision' she seems to have been afforded, to the opening of Chapter 15, where Adela and Aziz accompanied by a guide resume 'the slightly tedious expedition'. The chapter is short but important, for it conveys a clear picture of Adela's state of mind before she enters the cave. Silent at first, she thinks of Ronny and marriage, recognises that she does not love him or find him physically attractive, and wonders whether she should after all break off her engagement. She then asks Aziz about *his* marriage, and shocks him with the naïve enquiry whether he has more than one wife. She is still thinking of marriage when she enters the cave, and 'marriage' is the last word of the chapter. More confusions ensue as the next chapter (16) opens, for Aziz, deeply offended at her question, dives into one cave, she enters another, and the guide remains outside. When Aziz emerges he learns to his consternation that his guest has disappeared and may be lost in the maze of caves. Then, by a sudden twist and leap in the narrative that mirrors the suddenness and the bewildering nature of Aziz's discovery, he spots her, far below, 'speaking to another lady' who has conveniently arrived in a car. Aziz's mood, which has already changed from happiness to despair and from despair to puzzlement, now changes to exuberant delight. But the undercurrents of the scene are troubled: Fielding, who has arrived with the English party, senses that something is amiss, even though Aziz – more concerned with politeness than with accuracy – offers an explanation for Adela's abrupt departure. Mrs Moore is bored with Aziz, Fielding and the whole business, and has already begun her retreat from life. The journey back to Chandrapore is quickly narrated, and as the chapter draws to an end Forster's narrative takes another unexpected turn: Aziz is arrested at the station, damagingly attempts to escape and is led off to prison. The visit to the caves, which began as a gesture of friendship and a comedy of errors, has produced potentially tragic misunderstandings and threatens to widen the gulf between races still further.

With hindsight the reader comes to realise that he has been the victim of a narrator's trick: as in a detective story, the clues have been put into his hands but the interpretation of them withheld. The stages whereby Adela has been separated from her friends, has been left alone with Aziz, has suffered an unpleasant though undefined experience in the cave, and has abruptly been rescued (the familiar Forsterian device of the rescue party yet again), are in themselves innocent, the result of life's muddles; collectively they constitute an incriminating case against Aziz for anyone with an interest in giving them this interpretation. If he had systematically planned to assault her, or if some malevolent deity had plotted his downfall, things could hardly look worse for him, and it must be said that, as often, there is some contrivance and implausibility, reminiscent of Victorian fictional conventions, in Forster's plotting at this stage of the book. What 'plot', with its emphasis on explicable causal relationships, cannot explain, however, is precisely what Adela's experience has been, and in Forster's text this remains a mystery. Like Mrs Moore, she has been disturbed by the echo, though its effect on the two women has been quite different. The David Lean film, apparently distrustful of the unexplained, earlier interpolates a scene in which Adela encounters and flees from some erotic sculptures in a ruined temple, with the implication that her imagined experience in the caves was an expression of her fear of sexuality. This explicitness is alien to Forster's method, which consists in 'bouncing' the reader from one unexpected event to another in the disconcerting manner of life itself. He shows Adela, at the end of Chapter 15, entering the cave and 'wondering . . . about marriage', then turns to Aziz and offers no account of what has happened to her or any explanation of her abrupt departure, until Chapter 17. This abrupt switch in point of view leaves the reader sharing Aziz's ignorance and puzzlement.

In Chapter 17, the cause of Anglo-Indian friendship seems to have suffered a mortal blow: Turton tells Fielding sententiously that in twenty-five years' service in India he has 'never known anything but disaster result when English people and Indians attempt to be intimate socially'. Turton, imprisoned within his own incurable prejudices, relies on catch-phrases: the pseudo-poetic reference to 'an English girl fresh from England', which brings tears to his eyes, substitutes a fantasy-figure for the real Miss Quested, of whom the narrator remarks drily at the beginning of Chapter 20 that 'Although [she] had not made herself popular with the English, she brought out all that was fine in their character'. Fielding, in contrast, is 'after facts' and, guided by reason rather than prejudice and affection rather than dislike, is determined to establish the truth. In the meeting at the club (Ch. 20), Fielding courageously declares his belief in Aziz's innocence and thus isolates himself from the rest of the British community. If the novel has a hero, we may reflect at this point, Fielding has a strong claim to the title.

Aziz's arrest, and the charge of assault against him, polarises the community – a familiar gambit on the part of Forster, who is fond of presenting his characters with an issue that compels them to take sides. Events now move towards his trial in

Chapter 24. As we learn in Chapter 22, 'the machinery has started', and the metaphor is appropriate both to the legal and bureaucratic process and to the automatic quality of the main Anglo-Indian respose, for these are people who do not think out each issue as a unique moral problem but proceed by watchwords and stock responses. (The metaphor reappears at a significant moment near the end of Chapter 24, when the Superintendent regards Adela as 'a broken machine'.) In their different ways, however, Fielding, Mrs Moore and Adela all stand apart from this tribal unanimity. Fielding staunchly insists on his friend's innocence – he does not simply regard Aziz as a type but knows and respects him as an individual; Mrs Moore tells Adela that Aziz is innocent (but does so 'indifferently'); Adela finds herself caught between the older woman and Ronny, who (unsurprisingly) represents the hard Anglo-Indian line. Mrs Moore's indifference is an aspect of the profound change that has come over her since the visit to the caves and the mysterious and unsettling experience of the echo: her condition is one of cosmic depression, a state in which

> the horror of the universe and its smallness are both visible at the same time – the twilight of the double vision in which so many elderly people are involved. If this world is not to our taste, well, at all events there is Heaven, Hell, Annihilation. . . .
>
> What had spoken to her in that scoured-out cavity of the granite? What dwelt in the first of the caves? Something very old and very small. Before time, it was before space also. Something snub-nosed, incapable of generosity – the undying worm itself. (Ch. 23)

Persuaded by Ronny to return to England before the trial – an act later interpreted by the friends of Aziz as a conspiracy to suppress the truth – she is preparing to leave India, and the withdrawal of mind and body, it turns out, is a preparation for withdrawal from life itself by one who has become convinced that nothing in life has any meaning and nothing matters. As Colmer points out, though, this is not Forster's last word on Mrs Moore and her vision: the chapter ends, as her boat pulls out of Bombay harbour, on an unexpected note of affirmation:

As she drove through the huge city which the West has built and abandoned with a gesture of despair, she longed to stop, though it was only Bombay, and disentangle the hundred Indias that passed each other in its streets. The feet of the horses moved her on, and presently the boat sailed and thousands of coconut palms appeared all round the anchorage and climbed the hills to wave her farewell. 'So you thought an echo was India; you took the Marabar caves as final?' they laughed. 'What have we in common with them . . .?'

The vastness and vitality of India reassert themselves, its complexity defying easy judgments and even comprehension, and the despair that has been born of her experience in the caves – a despair involving a loss of faith in love and goodness, beauty and grandeur, in personal relationships and life itself – is revealed as only one aspect of a human experience that can also embrace a joyful acceptance of humanity (represented by the Bombay crowds) and the earth (the waving palms).

Absent in body, Mrs Moore remains a spiritual and even a ghostly presence at the trial scene in Chapter 24. Her name, 'Indianized into Esmiss Esmoor', becomes a kind of 'charm' or magic formula when chanted by the crowd outside the courtroom. Inside, as Adela gives her evidence, she does not merely remember but relives the expedition, and in a kind of splendid vision discovers the truth of what has happened, or not happened: 'she returned to the Marabar Hills, and spoke from them across a sort of darkness'. For all his blunders over court procedure, Forster handles the narrative and the human situations very skilfully, and there is genuine tension as the court, and the reader, hold their breath when Adela is asked whether Aziz followed her into the cave. With her negative, and her withdrawal of the charge, the scene ends in uproar – with Anglo-Indian fury, as her compatriots turn against the girl they have so recently sentimentalised as a heroine and a martyr, and in Indian jubilation. (In only one touch – 'Mrs Turton . . . gave [Ronny] an irritable blow, then screamed insults at Adela' – does Forster allow his prejudices to show and step over the bounds of psychological and social credibility.)

At least the scene almost ends there, but the final picture is in fact the very different one of the native pulling the punkah (the manually operated fan), who serenely continues his rhythmical task. He has appeared earlier, at the beginning of the courtroom scene, and the description of him there ('Almost naked', 'splendidly formed', like 'A god') is echoed at the end of the chapter ('the beautiful naked god'). It is a nice small-scale example of Forster's use of recurring symbolic detail to develop the pattern and design of his narrative: the man not only serves to frame the whole episode but suggests the qualities of an unchanging India in which the brief turmoil of such events as the Anglo-Indian campaign against Aziz are of no more account than the 'clouds of descending dust' stirred by the punkah.

The immediate public aftermath of the trial is a triumphal march, with Aziz as the hero of the hour, and a near-riot: the case has inevitably taken on political dimensions and the acquittal is seen as a blow to British prestige and authority. The private aftermath is Adela's discovery that the echo that has haunted her has disappeared, vanquished by her recognition of the truth as if the trial had been a course of psychoanalysis. In Chapter 26 Fielding, the rationalist, offers her an explanation of what happened in the caves: she was unwell at the time (she admits to a 'vague' uneasiness, 'a sort of sadness', dating from the time of the tea-party with Aziz and Godbole), suffered a hallucination, and broke the strap of the field-glasses herself. Or, he suggests, she may genuinely have been assaulted by the guide, who has never reappeared, or by a wandering stranger. In the courtroom scene, however, she has already gone halfway towards an explanation that makes perfectly good psychological sense:

> her disaster in the cave was connected, though by a thread, with another part of her life, her engagement to Ronny. She had thought of love just before she went in, and had innocently asked Aziz what marriage was like, and she supposed that her question had roused evil in him.

Only the last part of this is wrong: the 'evil' has come not from Aziz but from within herself and is the product not of anyone's deed but of the culture of her nation and class, English middle-class puritanism, which fears sex and is distrustful of love.

A more dramatic revelation is that Mrs Moore has died on the way home and was indeed already dead when her name was mentioned in court. The knowledge of this gives a retrospective ghostly quality to her role on that occasion, and as the news of her death spreads through Chandrapore she becomes the subject of legend (Ch. 28); even Fielding recognises that 'people are not really dead until they are felt to be dead', and 'Esmiss Esmoor' is still a felt presence. It is left to Aziz, who recalls that he saw her only three times (a magic number), to pronounce her epitaph: 'I know she is an Oriental' (Ch. 27). He uses the present tense because he has not yet heard of her death (Fielding breaks the news to him a moment later), but it also suggests that she remains a living reality (Aziz has said that he will seek her advice, and recalls that he 'fancied she was present' in court).

It is now Adela's turn to leave India: her engagement broken off, she begins the journey northwards (Ch. 29), and soon Fielding follows the same route; unlike Adela, however, he intends to return to India when his leave is over. Before his departure, a 'tragic coolness' (in Forster's slightly melodramatic phrase) develops between him and Aziz (Ch. 31): entirely groundless rumours that Fielding has been having an affair with Adela are believed by Aziz, who has 'no sense of evidence' (an odd racial generalisation on Forster's part) even though he is a scientist, and who is deeply hurt by what seems to him a betrayal. Impelled by his feelings rather than a realistic assessment of the situation – for he and Fielding, the 'blank, frank atheist', are poles apart temperamentally – he convinces himself that his friend will marry Adela and is suspicious of Fielding's motives for persuading him not to press for damages against Adela. Their parting is thus clouded by a sense of estrangement: human affairs are once again governed by muddle. The brief chapter (32) that ends Part II records the stages of Fielding's northward journey: India recedes, more temperate climates replace the torrid heat that has dominated this central portion of the novel, and the final phrase of the chapter (in this novel, often a position that bestows on words more weight than they normally sustain) shows him in England amid 'the buttercups and daisies of June'.

Part III, 'Temple', is by far the shortest of the three sections of the novel and occupies only about one-eighth of its total length. Colmer describes it as 'a brief coda that offers a muted epiphany and a partial reconciliation of the major discords of the novel'.[64] Forster himself felt that it was 'architecturally necessary' but, with hindsight, believed that 'there ought to be more after it.'[65] Whether it constitutes too little or too much, or is just right, is a matter for critical argument. It settles some questions of plot-interest (Fielding's marriage, for instance) that would otherwise be left unsettled but is in other respects inconclusive, even ambiguous. In any case, though, its function seems to have less to do with narrative than with symbol and pattern. The titles of the three parts of the novel, 'Mosque', 'Caves' and 'Temple', represent, respectively, the Muslim, British and Hindu elements in the Indian scene (the second perhaps symbolically caught between the others) and, as Forster pointed out, are also identified with the cold, hot and rainy seasons viewed symbolically as well as realistically. It is tempting to see this third portion as the synthesis reconciling the opposites of thesis and antithesis – presenting Hinduism, that is, as offering a serene harmonising of opposites and antagonisms – but the tone of these chapters, and the presentation of the religious festival and of Professor Godbole, make such an interpretation unconvincing. And as we shall see, the closing words of the novel deny any completeness of reconciliation or resolution of discords. Godbole's Hinduism stands for wholeness and universal love, but it remains an ideal and an aspiration rather than a living reality so far as the novel's main characters are concerned, and the book ends with qualified negatives rather than confident affirmations.

As the opening sentence of Part III makes clear, two years have passed since the events related at the end of Part II. Godbole 'stands in the presence of God', but the solemnity of the phrase is soon counterpointed by the comic absurdity of Godbole himself, the absent-minded professor of caricature, fumbling with his pince-nez. Yet he does have an impressive sense of religion as something that pervades and permeates life at the highest and lowest levels of experience, and neither the fact that he is a figure of fun nor some incongruities in the festival itself (the slip in the inscription of 'God si Love', the band playing a European waltz) can alter this. As Forster makes clear, what is in question is not the long-faced, black-clothed Sabbatarianism of English middle-class Christianity but a joyful acceptance of life in all its diversity, the trivial as well as the splendid (though strictly speaking there is nothing, not even an insect, that is trivial): to quote Colmer again, 'It is one of Forster's main themes that a religion or philosophy which claims to embrace all life must be able to accept the comic and the sublime, the muddle and the mystery'[66] (the last phrase echoing Forster's own in Chapter 29: 'Perhaps life is a mystery, not a muddle'). To love 'the whole universe', thus 'imitating God', is the ideal, and at the end of Chapter 33 Godbole recalls two images from his past experience – Mrs Moore and a wasp he has somewhere observed – and reflects that 'all he could do' is to love them equally. This is the affirmative aspect of a novel that, up to this point, has been largely concerned with the difficulties of loving one another.

In Chapter 34 Aziz learns that Fielding has returned from England, accompanied by 'His wife and her brother', and thereupon jumps to the conclusion that his former friend has married Adela Quested. Tearing up Fielding's letter, he resolves to have nothing to do with them: upon the mystery of the religious festival, everyday muddle has supervened. However, they soon meet by chance (Ch. 35), and after the misunderstanding has surfaced Aziz discovers that it is not Adela whom Fielding has married but Stella, Mrs Moore's daughter by her second marriage. A more conventional novelist would have seized the opportunity for a happy ending to the tragi-comedy of errors and have made this discovery set the seal on the friendship between the Englishman and the Indian, but Forster does not believe that life offers, and does not permit his fiction to present, such easy solutions. Aziz's embarrassment turns to anger, and he tells Fielding that he wishes 'no Englishman or Englishwoman to be my friend'. During his impassioned speech it rains heavily, and water flows indeed throughout this novel, from the Ganges and the 'ancient tanks' in the opening chapter to the 'tank' in the final sentence; the motif is especially prominent, however, in this third part and seems to carry religious associations of spiritual renewal and baptism into a new life. Its appearance in this scene of sad misunderstanding and destructive anger is therefore rather puzzling; perhaps the implication is that Aziz must purge his heart of hatred and resentment before he can attain the loving relationship that is ultimately possible. The road to this goal leads him through the discovery that Ralph Moore, Fielding's brother-in-law, is 'an Oriental' (like his mother) in his capacity to recognise a stranger as a friend (as she had done when she first met Aziz near the beginning of the novel); with 'a little shudder' Aziz recalls that he spoke exactly the same words to Mrs Moore in the mosque. He takes Ralph rowing (the water motif again), and after a collision the two of them, with Fielding and Stella, are all immersed as if in some cleansing ritual. Friendship and love are again possible: Aziz even writes to his former enemy, Adela, to thank her for her courage in telling the truth, and the misunderstandings and misery associated with the Marabar Caves seem finally to be 'wiped out'.

On a last ride before Fielding leaves, he and Aziz argue passionately about Indian independence and recognise that the time for real friendship between the races has not yet come. Fielding, with his optimistic faith in good sense and good intentions, is reluctant to admit that this is so, but part of the purpose of the novel is to expose the shortcomings of Fielding's kind of confident enlightened liberalism, and 'not yet' and 'not there' are the phrases that linger in the ear and the mind after the last words have been read. Forster himself has travelled a long way, in every sense, since he suggested in his early novels that all might be well if only Englishmen could bring themselves to behave like Italians, or public schoolmasters could imitate shepherds. The conclusion of *A Passage to India* is neither optimistic nor pessimistic but presents a clear-eyed, unillusioned acknowledgment of the vastness of the issues and the problems that render difficult – not impossible, but very difficult – the quest for universal brotherhood.

6

Minor Fiction: *Maurice* and the Short Stories

The five novels so far discussed constitute the main body of Forster's achievement but by no means the whole of it. To these central texts, which have long enjoyed classic status, must be added a sixth novel, a number of short stories and a considerable quantity of non-fictional writing in both longer and shorter forms, including biographies, travel books, a volume of criticism, an opera libretto, and a mass of journalism and occasional pieces – essays, broadcasts, reviews, lectures and the like – some of which is collected into two volumes but much of which remains uncollected. Considerations of 'major' and 'minor' inevitably arise; some readers, indeed, would wish to divide the five novels into two groups, with *Howards End* and *A Passage to India* as 'major' works and the others as 'minor' or 'lesser'. There is certainly a sense in which Forster's 'condition of England' novel and his exploration, both realistic and symbolic, of interracial relationships are more ambitious novels than their predecessors, though it goes without saying that the scale and programme of a work are not necessarily related to its artistic success. As already suggested in Chapter 1, however, it is one of Forster's characteristics that in the course of even some quite trivial, small-scale piece – a review of a bad book or a popular radio broadcast – his tone can suddenly deepen and some of his most passionately held principles be invoked. Like the Christian belief that judges every act, however commonplace, in the light of eternity, Forster's humanism constantly refers small issues to his basic moral and ethical convictions, though strictly speaking there are no such things as small issues. His practice constantly exemplifies the general truth enunciated by a great Victorian humanist, George Eliot, when she wrote in

Middlemarch that it is by 'these acts called trivialities' that human destinies are determined.

It follows from this that the distinction between major and minor writings is a somewhat artificial one, since a piece of journalism may touch on issues as momentous as a full-length novel: Forster's ideas and ideals do not go off duty when the literary occasion is a relatively unimportant one. But artistic success is, of course, another matter, and here discriminations are in order. This chapter will consider, quite briefly, the fictional writings which, while not without interest – Forster could be irritating or unconvincing but he was incapable of being boring – are exercises in minor genres or, in the case of his sixth novel, a major intention that turned into a minor achievement.

Forster's novel *Maurice* appeared in October 1971, sixteen months after his death, but its origins go back some sixty years. After the publication and notable success of *Howards End* in 1910, he seems to have experienced great difficulty in writing another novel and to have made more than one false start. (The fragmentary *Arctic Summer*, for instance, belongs to the spring of 1914.) But in a three-month period in late 1913, he wrote the first draft of the short novel that became *Maurice*. He revised it during the first half of the following year, and returned to his manuscript intermittently over the next half-century. Substantial revisions seem to have been made as late as 1960, at which time Forster wrote on the cover the words 'Publishable – but worth it?' Long before this date, the book had been read by various friends, but it became 'publishable' only towards the end of Forster's lifetime, after the recommendations of the Wolfenden Committee (1957) led to reforms in the laws relating to homosexual behaviour, thus both reflecting and promoting a changed climate of opinion, and the Obscene Publications Act (1959) liberalised what had effectively been a situation of unofficial censorship that extended to serious works of literature. It is important to remember that *Maurice* was written, and restricted to private circulation for several decades, in a context of social and legal intolerance of the homosexual relationships that are its subject.

When it did appear, many readers were disappointed and typical critical verdicts were 'ill-written', 'deeply embarrassing' and 'deeply flawed'. Walter Allen shrewdly commented that it suffers from 'over-concentration on a single issue',[67] and related to this is the marked contrast in texture with Forster's other fiction: whereas his other novels are by turns wittily ironic and socially observant, richly symbolic and even (especially in *The Longest Journey*) romantic to the point of lushness, *Maurice* is spare, restrained, laconic, somewhat dry and even banal in places. It is a short novel but contains a large number (46) of mainly very short chapters, some of them of less than a page; it works through brief episodes and the dialogue is at times almost telegraphic. Lytton Strachey, who read the manuscript and commented perceptively on it in a letter to Forster (12 March 1915; reprinted in *E. M. Forster: The Critical Heritage*), described one passage as 'staccato' in style. The number of major characters is restricted to three, of whom one does not appear until two-thirds of the way through the book. Also, most uncharacteristically, it is without humour.

Yet *Maurice* is the work of an experienced novelist and we are left with the choice of regarding it as an experiment that misfired or of supposing that Forster knew exactly what he was about – that the flatness, the avoidance of eloquence and colour, proceed from a deliberate attempt to play down the sensationalism inherent in the theme, to present the situation as if it were ordinary, to let it speak for itself. If the alternative was rhetoric, sentimentality and overt propagandising, the decision may after all have been a wise one. But there may, of course, have been other alternatives that Forster lacked the vision or the courage to contemplate.

Forster sets himself a difficult problem at the outset by presenting a hero who is, as we learn on the first page, 'not in any way remarkable'. Maurice Hall is uniformly commonplace: athletic, handsome, inarticulate, a successful businessman, he seems at first to belong, like Gerald in *The Longest Journey*, to the large tribe of insensitive middle-class English philistines. What makes him interesting is his homosexuality, and Forster seems to have tried to avoid the charge of special pleading by creating a protagonist as different from himself as possible in all respects save one. From his public school, where it is necessary to be 'cruel and rude' in order to survive (qualities that Forster must have observed and suffered from, though hardly emulated, at Tonbridge), Maurice proceeds to Cambridge and there comes under the influence of Greek culture and thought, with its

ideals of tolerance and sexual freedom, and is introduced to
Plato's *Symposium* by a new friend, Clive Durham, who falls in
love with him and persuades him to abandon the religious
beliefs, conventional rather than fervent, in which he has been
brought up.

In his 'Terminal Note', dated September 1960 and of great
interest for its account of the creative origins of this novel,
Forster says that 'Clive is Cambridge'. Clearly, too, there are
elements of self-portraiture in this character and it is notable
that these elements have been displaced from the central
character, where one might more naturally expect to find them,
to a secondary figure.

Clive's love, however, is romantic and idealistic in nature; it
is the taller, stronger and more athletic Maurice who desires
physical fulfilment. But the narrator puts such desires in their
place in Chapter 15: 'he was too young to detect the triviality of
contact for contact's sake', and the 'love scene' in the following
chapter is spiritual rather than physical. In a novel intended to
strike a blow for the legitimacy of homosexual relationships,
this renunciation of the flesh seems curiously self-denying and
perhaps represents a failure of nerve on Forster's part.

Part Two repeats some of the earlier narrative, this time from
the point of view of Clive. Guilt-ridden by his sexual desires, he
is liberated by reading Plato, but derives from the *Phaedrus* not
a licence to *act* spontaneously but a freedom to idealise
homosexual love. After leaving Cambridge, the two friends
enjoy an 'affectionate and consistent' relationship (Chapter 18)
for a time, but by the end of Part Two, in an unusual form of
the 'conversion' motif favoured by Forster, Clive has turned to
heterosexuality and later marries. It is now Maurice's turn to
discover his own nature – a slow process, and one that takes
him in a different direction from Clive, since Maurice's nature
is physical rather than idealistic. His upbringing, of course, has
conditioned him to be ashamed of 'lust', and the last third of
the book traces the re-education of his heart (another favourite
Forsterian theme, and a traditionally dominant one in the
English novel) – 'the flesh educating the spirit'. This is brought
about by his love for Alec Scudder, a gamekeeper. Alec's
occupation associates him with the outdoors and the natural
world, and he provides a liberating contrast to the indoor world
of Maurice's friends of his own social class: when he first sees

Alec, Maurice is leaning out of a window and finds himself 'star[ing] straight into the bright brown eyes of a young man' standing outside; in the next chapter (37), Maurice meets Alec twice in a garden, and the episodes contain many uninsistent and effective symbolic touches and details at once realistic and suggestive (for example, Maurice's formal dress, Alec's corduroys; the pollen of evening primroses that powders Maurice's hair and leads a fellow-guest to describe him, with unconscious accuracy, as 'bacchanalian').

The class difference between Maurice and Alec is, strictly speaking, irrelevant: if Maurice's task is to find himself through a full recognition of his own nature and a wholly satisfying relationship, there seems to be no reason why this should not be accomplished through a man of his own class. But for Forster, as for more outspoken campaigners of his generation such as Edward Carpenter, the sexual and the socio-political issues are closely related. (Carpenter, who has been referred to in Chapter 1, was a socialist intellectual who lived with a young man of the working class; his influence on Forster, who stated on one occasion that Carpenter 'preferred the working classes to his own',[68] was considerable.) It is as if the two kinds of emancipation, while not necessarily interdependent, have the effect of reinforcing each other and strengthen the defiance of conventional prejudices; also, perhaps, Forster found it easier to shed the bonds that tied him to the manners and outlook of his own class with someone from a different class – or at least to imagine doing so. (We recall that, early and late, his own intense relationships tended to be with those who were outside his own class, or foreigners, or both.)

Yet another factor is involved, moreover, for Alec is not only a member of the lower class: he also represents a pre-industrial and anti-urban way of life, 'the life of the earth'. (Here we may be reminded of Stephen Wonham in *The Longest Journey* and of Forster's short story 'Ansell', and may recall that Carpenter cultivated the simple life half a century before 'alternative life-styles' became fashionable.) Again, there seems to be no necessary connection between these elements: Maurice's friend might plausibly have been a factory worker. But Forster seems intent upon linking ideas that do not inevitably exist in conjunction with each other: the homosexual's search for a permanent relationship and a way of life; the flight from contemporary society, the mechanised world and the city (Maurice turns to the 'greenwood' and exchanges stockbroking for manual labour); and the breaking down of class barriers. Lytton Strachey told Forster that 'the Class question' was in his view 'rather a red herring',[69] and the present-day reader may well be troubled by similar doubts.

Maurice has two endings. The original one affords a glimpse into the future and depicts a chance meeting in Yorkshire (where, perhaps not coincidentally, Carpenter and his lover lived) between a minor character and two woodsmen, with the implicit guarantee of an enduring relationship. This may have seemed to Forster, on later reflection, sentimental and facile; at any rate he substituted an ending which does not look to the future and promises no permanence in the relationship between Maurice and Alec, but allows Maurice to speak with unprecedented eloquence to Clive, who is shown as trapped in a dull marriage, about his love for Alec, and to bid farewell to the life he is quitting. Like much else in the novel, this ending divided Forster's critics; again it has to be said that the case has been weakened by special pleading (Clive's marriage, for example, can hardly be taken as an indictment of all marriages – and it is in any case a marriage in all but the most literal sense that is in question between the lovers).

Maurice is an Edwardian novel published in the late twentieth century, and inevitably the 'period' quality makes itself felt in the social world inhabited by the characters: Maurice's Cambridge, to take an obvious example, is very much the Cambridge of Forster's own undergraduate years, and the young men speak a class dialect that sometimes has a flavour as archaic as that of Kipling's schoolboy stories. Nor is the boldness of theme matched by a boldness of language: Forster ventures upon no linguistic experiments of the kind that made that other novel about an escape to the greenwood, Lawrence's *Lady Chatterley's Lover*, notorious but observes a scrupulous decorum and uses no word that might bring a blush to the cheek of an Edwardian housemaster (masturbation, for example, is coyly referred to as 'the practices he had abandoned as a boy' and 'acts [bringing] more fatigue than pleasure'). Sexual acts remain shadowy and unconvincing; and Forster must be judged as having failed to devise a language appropriate to his subject-matter. This failure is symptomatic of the novel as a whole, which is more courageous in conception than in execution. *Maurice* is inevitably of great interest to the student of Forster but only a limited success as a work of fiction.

As well as his six novels, Forster wrote a number of short stories. Two collections that appeared in his lifetime, *The Celestial Omnibus* (1911) and *The Eternal Moment* (1928), were conflated in his later years as *The Collected Short Stories* (1947), in the introduction to which Forster refers to the contents as 'all that I have accomplished in a particular line'. After his death it became clear that this statement was misleading, for in 1972 his literary executors published *The Life to Come*, which contains fourteen largely unpublished fictional pieces. Forster evidently destroyed a number, perhaps a fairly large number, of stories: in his diary for 8 April 1922, for instance, at about the time he again took up *A Passage to India*, he noted that he had just 'burnt my indecent writings' because he believed that they 'clogged me artistically'. According to his friend Joe Ackerley, there was another bonfire in the early 1960s of the stories deemed unworthy of posthumous publication.[70] Like *Maurice*, these stories, or some of them, had circulated among Forster's friends.

The contents of the *Collected Short Stories* belong to his earlier period: most of them had been originally published in Edwardian periodicals and they bear the stamp of their period and genre. Some contain echoes or anticipations of his longer works of fiction, and one early critic, Rose Macaulay, described them as 'abstracts and brief chronicles of the earlier novels'.[71] Many resort to the supernatural or the whimsical, and a recurring theme is the way in which the forces of nature, especially as personified in the mythological figure of the god Pan, assert themselves in modern life and shatter the timidities and hypocrisies of conventional existence. This celebration of the Dionysiac, usually in a Home Counties setting, is often self-consciously literary and, again, 'period' in quality, though the best of the stories, such as 'The Road from Colonus', transcend the occasional archness and bookishness and still have power: the economy forced on the writer of a short story sharpens Forster's irony, intensifies the drama of his situations and makes his symbolism more pointed.

In contrast, *The Life to Come* contains stories that range in date from Forster's youth to his old age. 'Ansell', which was written in 1902 or 1903, must be one of his earliest attempts at fiction; there are stories from the 1920s and 1930s; and the finest story in the volume, 'The Other Boat', belongs to 1957–8. Some (e.g. 'The Obelisk') are light-hearted jokes, rather coyly indecent and presumably written for fun and perhaps for self-stimulation. 'The Other Boat', however, is an impressively tragic tale, masterly in its sureness of touch and a worthy pendant to *A Passage to India*. One outstanding short story does not place Forster among the great practitioners of that form, but no student of his work ought to miss the stories, which are characteristic in many ways – of his weaknesses as well as his strengths.

Conclusion

Forster's contribution to the tradition of the novel was not that of a great innovator or experimentalist: his most ambitious novel, *A Passage to India*, belongs to the same decade as *Women in Love*, *Ulysses* and *Mrs Dalloway*, but it is a more traditional work than any of these. In many respects he is closer to the great nineteenth-century novelists than to the most historically significant of his own contemporaries, though he was certainly not unaware or unappreciative of what the latter were doing (he was, for instance, one of Lawrence's earliest defenders). It should not be supposed, however, that he merely galvanised a moribund form into temporarily renewed activity: the tradition that he helped to revitalise and perpetuate is one that continued throughout the twentieth century alongside the more institutionally celebrated traditions of modernism and post-modernism, and later novelists such as Christopher Isherwood and Angus Wilson have made no secret of their debt to Forster.

Forster said that he learned from Jane Austen 'the possibilities of domestic humour',[72] but important though this confession is, it acknowledges only a part of the legacy he inherited from his nineteenth-century predecessors. In his exploration of limited social and personal themes and settings as paradigms to suggest universal moral and ethical problems, and in his unblushing use of the narrator as preacher and mentor, he is closer to George Eliot than to such contemporaries as James Joyce and Virginia Woolf. Like Eliot, he is not concerned only with the novel as aesthetic object, game or technical problem, but regards it as his Evangelical forbears might have regarded a sermon or a serious essay, as a way of making the world a better place.

At the same time, he was a born novelist in his fascination with individuality – with the quirks and oddities, whether lovable or deplorable, or simply viewed as objects of anthropological curiosity, of human beings regarded not in the mass but one at a time. This again is an interest in 'message' rather than 'medium' and his contribution to the technique of the novel was not of first-rate importance. His experiments with symbolism and narrative method, for example, though they are important elements in any reading of his work, are not on the scale of such contemporaries as Conrad or Ford Madox Ford. He is, however, a writer remarkable for the distinctiveness and power of his vision and voice; without cultivating (except occasionally, and sometimes disastrously) a wilful eccentricity of style, he wrote a prose that is unmistakable even in small quantities: he is one of those writers whom, as one reads them, one can nearly always *hear* – a living voice, flexible, responsive and considering, behind the rigidities of the printed text.

When most Edwardian fiction is virtually unreadable and deservedly forgotten, his novels retain a remarkable freshness even after many re-readings, and new generations of readers, for whom the social world of which he wrote is almost as remote as that of the Victorians or even the Augustans, respond with pleasure to his wit and irony. In his alliance of comedy and satire with the realistic tradition and with consistent moral seriousness, Forster stands almost alone among the major novelists of our century.

Notes

1. P. N. Furbank and F. J. H. Haskell, 'The art of fiction I: E. M. Forster', *Paris Review* I (1953), 40.

2. P. N. Furbank, *E. M. Forster, A Life: Volume One, The Growth of the Novelist (1879–1914)* (London: Secker & Warburg, 1977), p. 28. (This volume is hereafter cited as *Life I*.)

3. *Life I*, p. 22.

4. *Life I*, p. 34.

5. *Life I*, p. 37.

6. *My Sister and Myself: The Diaries of J. R. Ackerley*, ed. Francis King (London: Hutchinson, 1982), p. 45 (diary entry dated 4 December 1948).

7. *Life I*, p. 54.

8. John Colmer, *E. M. Forster: The Personal Voice* (London: Routledge & Kegan Paul, 1975), p. 7.

9. Ibid., p. 8.

10. *Life I*, p. 98.

11. *Life I*, pp. 122, 138.

12. Philip Gardner (ed.), *E. M. Forster: The Critical Heritage* (London: Routledge & Kegan Paul, 1973), pp. 12, 14.

13. *Life I*, p. 190.

14. *Life I*, p. 204.

15. Samuel Hynes, *The Edwardian Turn of Mind* (Princeton University Press, 1968), p. 150.

16. Gilbert Beith (ed.), *Edward Carpenter: An Appreciation* (London: Allen & Unwin, 1931), pp. 76, 80.

17. Frederick C. Crews, *E. M. Forster: The Perils of Humanism* (Princeton University Press, 1962), p. 3.

18. P. N. Furbank, *E. M. Forster, A Life: Volume Two, Polycrates' Ring (1914–1970)* (London: Secker & Warburg, 1978), p. 131. (This volume is hereafter cited as *Life II*.)

19. *Life II*, p. 132.

20. V. S. Pritchett, 'The Private Voice', *The Tale-Bearers* (New York: Vintage Books, 1981), p. 64. *Life II*, p. 277.

21. *Life II*, p. 279.

22. Angus Wilson, 'A conversation with E. M. Forster', *Encounter*, IX (1957), 53.

23. *Life II*, p. 309.

24. Ibid.

25. E. M. Forster, *Goldsworthy Lowes Dickinson* (London: Arnold, 1934), pp. 132, 147.

26. Oliver Stallybrass, Editor's Introduction to *Where Angels Fear to Tread* (London: Arnold, 1975), p. viii.

27. Quoted by Stallybrass, p. viii.

28. Ibid., p. ix.

29. Lionel Trilling, *E. M. Forster* (London: Hogarth Press, 1967), p. 52.

30. F. R. Leavis, 'E. M. Forster', *The Common Pursuit* (Harmondsworth: Penguin, 1976), p. 262; Colmer, p 56.

31. Crews, p. 74.

32. For full information on these early versions, see *The Lucy Novels: Early Sketches for 'A Room with a View'* (London: Arnold, 1977). See also Elizabeth Ellem's article in *Times Literary Supplement*, 28 May 1971.

33. *Life I*, pp. 83, 86–7; Colmer, p. 42.

34. *Life I*, p. 154.

35. K. W. Gransden, *E. M. Forster* (Edinburgh: Oliver & Boyd, 1962), p. 31.

36. Colmer, *The Personal Voice* p. 65; Gransden, p. 38; Trilling, p. 67; Rex Warner, *E. M. Forster* (London: Longmans, Green, 1950), p. 18; W. J. Harvey, 'Imagination and moral theme in E. M. Forster's *The Longest Journey*', *Essays in Criticism*, VI (1956), 432–3; *Life I*, p. 119.

37. *Life I*, p. 37. Forster's remarks on the prototypes of Cadover and Mrs Failing occur in his introduction, reprinted in the Abinger Edition of *The Longest Journey* (London: Arnold, 1984), which also includes other useful background material.

38. *Life I*, pp. 116–17.

39. *Life I*, p. 117.

40. S. P. Rosenbaum, '*The Longest Journey*: E. M. Forster's refutation of idealism', *E. M. Forster: A Human Exploration*, ed. G. K. Das and John Beer (London: Macmillan, 1979), p. 33.

41. *Selected Letters of E. M. Forster, Volume I: 1879–1920*, ed. Mary Lago and P. N. Furbank (London: Collins, 1983), p. 83.

42. Trilling, p. 67.

43. Leavis, p. 266.

44. *Athenaeum*, 18 May 1907; reprinted in *E. M. Forster: The Critical Heritage*, p. 87.

45. Peter Widdowson, *E. M. Forster's 'Howards End': Fiction as History* (Sussex University Press, 1977), p. 20.

46. Trilling, p. 99; Leavis, pp. 268–9. Trilling later gave the preference to *A Passage to India*, however: see Oliver Stallybrass's introduction to the Abinger Edition of *Howards End* (London: Arnold, 1978), p. xvi.

47. *Life I*, p. 103.

48. Colmer, *The Personal Voice*, p. 86.

49. Widdowson, p. 21.

50. Stallybrass, introduction to *Howards End*, p. vii.

51. *Life I*, pp. 161–2.

52. Stallybrass, introduction to *Howards End*, p. xvii.

53. R. N. Parkinson, 'The inheritors; or a single ticket for Howards End', *E. M. Forster: A Human Exploration*, p. 60.

54. Trilling, p. 99.

55. Warner, p. 21.

56. *The Manuscripts of Howards End*, ed. Oliver Stallybrass (London: Arnold, 1973), pp. xiii–xiv, 355.

57. For a hostile judgment on the language of this novel, however, see D. Maskell, 'Style and symbolism in *Howards End*', *Essays in Criticism*, xix (1969), 292–307. Maskell finds Forster 'insensitive . . . towards language', compares the hay-symbolism unfavourably with the hay-cutting scene in Tolstoi's *Anna Karenina*, and describes Forster's novel as 'a dead book . . . dead to the living surface of things. . . we know it is dead by its language'.

58. Stallybrass, introduction to *Howards End*, p. xvii.

59. In *E. M. Forster: The Critical Heritage*, p. 21.

60. Quoted by Colmer, *The Personal Voice*, p. 156.

61. In a 1952 interview (see note 1 above), Forster said he was 'pleased' when a critic 'noticed that the wasp upon which Godbole meditates during the festival . . . had already appeared earlier in the novel' (p. 39).

62. *Letters I*, p. 140.

63. Colmer, *the Personal Voice*, p. 158.

64. John Colmer, *E. M. Forster, 'A Passage to India'* (London: Arnold, 1967), p. 57.

65. Furbank and Haskell, p. 33.

66. Colmer, *E. M. Forster, 'A Passage to India'*, p. 58.

67. *Daily Telegraph*, 7 October 1971; reprinted in *E. M. Forster: The Critical Heritage*, p. 438.

68. *Freedom of Expression*, ed. H. Ould (London: Hutchinson, 1944), p. 13.

69. *E. M. Forster: The Critical Heritage*, p. 430. (Strachey is of course referring to the original version of the novel.)

70. *The Letters of J. R. Ackerley*, ed. Neville Braybrooke (London: 1975), p. 260.

71. Rose Macaulay, *The Writings of E. M. Forster* (London: Hogarth Press), p. 33.

72. Furbank and Haskell, p. 39.

Select Bibliography

FORSTER'S PRINCIPAL WRITINGS

Where Angels Fear to Tread (1905)
The Longest Journey (1907)
A Room with a View (1908)
Howards End (1910)
The Celestial Omnibus and Other Stories (1911)
Alexandria: A History and a Guide (1922)
Pharos and Pharillon (1923)
A Passage to India (1924)
Aspects of the Novel (1927)
The Eternal Moment and Other Stories (1928)
Goldsworthy Lowes Dickinson (1934)
Abinger Harvest (1936)
Two Cheers for Democracy (1951)
The Hill of Devi (1953)
Marianne Thornton, 1797–1887: A Domestic Biography (1956)
Maurice (1970)
The Life to Come (1971)

SELECTED CRITICISM

Place of publication is London unless indicated.

Rukun Advani, *E. M. Forster as Critic* (1985)
J. B. Beer, *The Achievement of E. M. Forster* (1962)
J. B. Beer (ed.), *'A Passage to India': Essays in Interpretation* (1986)
Glen Cavaliero, *A Reading of E. M. Forster* (1979)
John Colmer, *E. M. Forster: The Personal Voice* (1975)
Frederick C. Crews, *E. M. Forster: The Perils of Humanism* (Princeton, New Jersey, 1962)
G. K. Das, *E. M. Forster's India* (1977)
David Dowling, *Bloomsbury Aesthetics and the Novels of Forster and Woolf* (1985)
Christopher Gillie, *A Preface to Forster* (1983)
K. W. Gransden, *E. M. Forster* (Edinburgh, 1962)
J. S. Herz and R. K. Martin (eds.), *E. M. Forster: Centenary Revaluations* (1982)

J. K. Johnstone, *The Bloomsbury Group* (1954)

F. P. W. McDowell, *E. M. Forster* (New York, 1969)

J. S. Martin, *E. M. Forster: The Endless Journey* (1976)

Norman Page, *E. M. Forster's Posthumous Fiction* (Victoria, British Columbia, 1977)

P. J. M. Scott, *E. M. Forster: Our Permanent Contemporary* (1984)

Oliver Stallybrass (ed.), *Aspects of E. M. Forster* (1969)

Wilfred Stone, *The Cave and the Mountain: A Study of E. M. Forster* (1966)

Lionel Trilling, *E. M. Forster: A Study* (1943; rev. edn 1967)

Rex Warner, *E. M. Forster* (1950)

Alan Wilde (ed.), *Critical Essays on E. M. Forster* (Boston, Mass., 1985)

B. J. Kirkpatrick's *A Bibliography of E. M. Forster* (1965; rev. edn 1968) is especially valuable for the information it contains on Forster's numerous minor writings. F. P. W. McDowell's *E. M. Forster: An Annotated Bibliography of Writings about him* (Northern Illinois University Press, 1976) is a useful guide to the vast field of Forster criticism. On his contemporary reception, Philip Gardner's *E. M. Forster: The Critical Heritage* (1973) can be strongly recommended. As a biography of Forster, P. N. Furbank's *E. M. Forster: A Life* in two volumes (1977, 1978) is unlikely to be superseded. The Abinger Edition, edited by the late Oliver Stallybrass, includes not only definitive editions of Forster's major writings but also significant manuscript material.

Index